The Case for B2B Branding:

Pulling Away from the Business to Business Pack

First Edition

Bob Lamons

THOMSON

Australia · Brazil · Canada · Mexico · Singapore · Spain · United Kingdom · United States

THOMSON

SOUTH-WESTERN

The Case for B2B Branding, First Edition
Bob Lamons

For more information about our products, contact us at:

Thomson Learning
Academic Resource Center

1-800-423-0563

Thomson Higher Education
5191 Natorp Boulevard
Mason, Ohio 45040
USA

This book is dedicated to the two most important women in my life:

My mother, Evelyn, who taught me the importance of curiosity,

And my wife, Margaret, who taught me the value of lasting friendships.

TABLE OF CONTENTS

THE CASE STUDIES

ABOUT THE AUTHOR

Bob Lamons is President of Robert Lamons & Associates, a branding and b-to-b marketing communications firm located in Granbury, Texas. He can be reached at 817-279-7996 or lamons@ads2biz.com

ACKNOWLEDGEMENTS

It took almost three years to write this book. I'm indebted to so many people who helped and it would be impossible to thank each one individually. If your name's in the book, then you helped and I'm very grateful. I'm also grateful to lots of people whose names are not in the book—either they wanted it that way, or it just wasn't necessary in telling the story.

Many of the people I started working with moved on to other opportunities while the book was in progress, and I had to start fresh with their successors when I called later to get additional information or permission to use a visual. While that caused my anxiety level to temporarily shoot up, there was actually no reason to worry because everyone eventually helped me get what I needed.

Many business books don't have visuals, and now I know why. It's a pain in the you-know-what to get permission to reprint things. In some cases, you not only have to get permission from the agency and client, but also the photographer and even the people who appeared in the ad. The older the ad is, the harder it is to track down all the interested parties.

But still, this book is full of interesting visuals that will help you better understand what was done and how. So I'm very pleased about that.

Finally, I'd like to thank a small group of industry leaders who took the time to read my manuscript and give me feedback: Kevin Clancy, Rick Kean, Bob Lauterborn, Ralph Oliva, Al Ries, Randall Rothenberg, Rick Segal and Don Schultz—I can't tell you how much it meant to me. You guys are great.

PART ONE
THE SEVEN STEPS

CHAPTER 1

INTRODUCTION

W hen I started writing monthly columns for *Marketing News* back in 1992, it was always in the back of my mind that I would write a book some day. By forcing myself to submit my ideas and opinions to a regular forum that received scrutiny from the world's best marketing and advertising professionals, surely a book would emerge over time.

And ten years later, when I decided to get out of the ad agency rat race, the first thing I did was review the many dozens of topics I had written about to find the "hidden" book in that heaping mound of wisdom. It wasn't there.

MY GE EPIPHANY

There was, however, a topic worthy for a book, one that I had written about passionately and frequently. You might say I had my personal epiphany about branding at a marketing conference in 1999 when I heard a talk by Richard Costello, who was manager of marketing communications for General Electric at that time.

Costello stood in that large auditorium full of advertising and marketing professionals and uttered these immortal words, "General Electric generates *incremental* revenue of ten billion dollars every year due to the power of our brand." That's billion, not million. And it's incremental, meaning it just comes along for the ride. A bonus, if you will.

I'm sure those words went racing by most of the people in that room, because we're used to hearing big numbers from big company guys. But they hit me right between the eyes. How could it be true? How could a brand make such a difference for any company?

Costello went on to cite some examples like engineered plastics and jet engines where GE exerts considerable marketing leverage due to its reputation, broad product line and trusted technology.

GE's Lexan® performance polymers, for example, have long enjoyed price premiums, and Lexan brand power has opened the door to exclusive working relationships with plastics molders, automotive manufacturers and consumer electronics companies. When Apple rocked the computer world with its brightly colored "iMac" computers, GE worked closely with them and gave them a one year exclusive on the color palette.

SOFT WHITE LIGHT BULBS

But the example I remember best from Costello's presentation is the simplest one—for GE Soft White light bulbs. Light bulbs have been around since 1879. It's one of our most common household items—everybody knows what they are and how to use them (even how many ethnic minority type people it takes to screw one in).

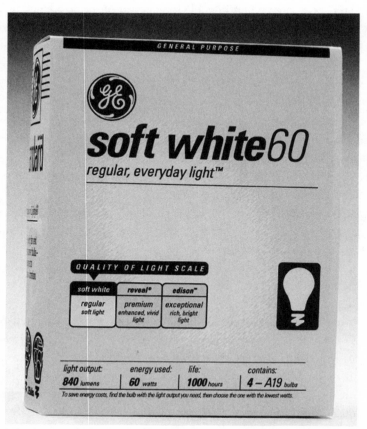

All light bulbs would appear to be the same, but most people pick GE because they think it's a better value. Used with permission.

Light bulbs are the opposite of rocket science. If there was ever a situation where you might assume all the manufacturing secrets have been fully revealed and analyzed, it would have to be light bulbs.

And yet, when you walk in a grocery store and go to the light bulb section, there you'll find GE Soft White bulbs proudly displayed next to competitive light bulbs and the generic store brand. The performance specifications are identical. The store brand is usually about a third less, but amazingly, most people reach for the GE brand.

Why is that? Do we have money to burn? Have we taken temporary leave of our senses? Or is it because we think the GE product represents the better buy? Maybe we think the GE bulbs will last longer or burn brighter.

Costello says the bottom line is trust. Trust is a vitally important part of the GE brand image. It's why you'll find the same GE brand on everything from appliances to medical imaging equipment. My dental plan is even from GE.

EXPECTATIONS ARE THE ESSENCE OF BRANDING

When you see the General Electric "meatball" as it is affectionately known, you immediately assume the product or service bearing that symbol is trustworthy. Expectations are, in fact, the essence of branding. A good brand will generate a highly focused set of expectations for the buyer, as well as for distributors, retailers, suppliers, employees and other audiences in your marketing universe.

If people see or hear your name and fail to conjure up any specific expectations, you have a brand problem.

Obviously, it's a lot more likely that large companies with their massive advertising budgets will have focused brand images, but don't assume this to be true. As you will see in this book, small companies can play the branding game, too. And large companies don't always play it very well.

As you compare the case studies described in the following chapters to your own situation and to those companies closest to you, you'll probably conclude that branding success doesn't come automatically — you have to work at it. In some cases, overcoming decades of neglect and empire-building within companies makes the job even harder.

KEEPING IT SIMPLE

One thing I am going to do for you, however, is to make it easier by stripping away the many pounds of branding jargon that most brand experts seem to think is necessary. Many of the serious authors in the branding field have defined terms so minutely that you find yourself going back repeatedly to previous pages just to be sure you comprehend the intended meaning.

My experience in more than thirty years of working with business-to-business (B2B) marketing and sales managers is that you have to keep things simple. I remember returning excitedly from a conference many years ago to my job as marketing communications manager for a Houston-based chemical company with an armload full of workbooks describing a new approach to budgeting.

I eagerly wrote a cover memo and distributed the workbooks to all my product and marketing managers, asking them to read the information and fill in the prescribed data so that follow-up meetings could be scheduled. Not even 24-hours passed before I was called on the carpet by the marketing V.P. to explain myself.

In addition to requiring them to learn something new, it seems I had also broken the "we don't do things that way here" rule. My primary mistake, of course, was not going to visit with each manager personally. But as I discovered later, even that approach would have failed because the new budgeting method I was proposing was too complicated.

Even if I had personally walked them through every step, I still would've lost them before we reached the finish line. The subject matter exceeded their interest by too wide a margin.

So I'm going to do everything I can to keep this simple. Branding is too important to business-to-business marketers for us to keep acting like it isn't.

SEVEN STEPS TO BRAND BUILDING

The following chapters outline seven (and-a-half) simple steps to effective brand image management. These steps are, by design, fairly broad because I've learned there's no one right way to do this. If you line up one hundred "self proclaimed" branding experts in a room (and believe me, that wouldn't be difficult to do), you'll hear a hundred different branding processes described.

In the end, however, branding comes down to common sense, introspective thinking and roll-up-the-sleeves hard work.

It won't happen overnight, either. Brand image development takes years to accomplish because it takes place in the minds of your customers, suppliers and other audiences.

It's a difficult concept to accept that you don't actually "own" your brands. You own trademarks, and you have certain legal rights to protect and control the way your brands are promoted in the marketplace.

Step 1	Effective Teamwork
Step 2	Brand Architecture
Step 3	Audience Identification
Step 4	Brand Positioning
Step 5	Brand Personality
Step 5-1/2	Personality Makeovers
Step 6	Consistent Execution
Step 7	Brand Equity

Figure 1   The Seven And-a-half Steps To Branding Success.

But since brands reside in your customer's brains, you lose control at some point along the way. You can't force customers to accept the image you want. They'll get it when they're good and ready to get it, and not a minute sooner.

As my friend, Ralph Oliva, Executive Director of the Institute For The Study Of Business Markets at Penn State says, "Brands are what the market gives you back. Playing the game isn't easy, because you play it across the gulf between you and your markets."

But if you persevere and stay the course, the reward will be well worth the effort. Your focused brand image makes it easier for your customers to understand what they can expect from your company, which, in turn, will separate your organization from the competitive pack and provide leverageable marketing advantages.

The bottom line is that brands are potentially the most valuable assets any company can have. Consumer and retail marketers have known this for years. Many business-to-business marketers, unfortunately, are just now coming around to that reality.

Maybe it's time you had a branding epiphany. I hope so. There are lots of good stories in this book to help you along the way. So let's get started.

CHAPTER 2

STEP ONE

EFFECTIVE TEAMWORK

Okay, let's assume for the moment that you are at least holding out the possibility of finding value in a branding program for business-to-business products and services. You don't have to be totally sold on the concept yet, because we're going to examine a number of case studies and other pieces of evidence as we go. You'll have plenty of time to jump onboard the train if you'll just jog along with me for a while.

The first step in developing a business-to-business branding program is to get the key people involved and committed. As Jim Collins said in *Good To Great*, you need to get the right people on the bus, and it definitely starts at the top. A company's number one brand champion has got to be the CEO, followed closely by the CFO and CMO.

THE CEO AS BRAND CHAMPION

We'll talk in this chapter about who else should be on the team and what each person's contribution should be, but let's start with the CEO. I once wrote a *Marketing News* column about the one question a lowly marcom manager should ask the CEO if he or she was suddenly granted a surprise audience with His Eminence. (It could be *Her Eminence*, but the great majority of CEO's are men, so for the sake of convenience let's stick with the male gender reference.)

In approaching His Eminence, you could seek some positive feedback on your latest ad campaign or trade show promotion. By asking the Big Guy about that, you'd have the opportunity to explain how crucial you were to the whole process and build yourself up in his eyes.

But talking about your recent successes is pretty self-serving, and what if he didn't particularly like your creative efforts? That would send the conversation immediately down the drain with no easy recovery. So it's best to steer clear of stuff like that.

9

As I concluded in that article several years ago, the best question to ask the CEO, is "in five words or less, what is the brand image you'd like for our company to have?"

Notice I didn't ask about the vision statement. Every company has one of course, and the CEO can explain it in excruciating detail. But he's the only one who can. Customers certainly don't care about your vision statement, and they're not about to give you credit for being the "Number One provider with the highest quality and greatest return on investment, employing the most dedicated people who make products that are good for mankind and the environment." That's just not gonna happen.

Cartoonist and noted business philosopher Scott Adams has ridiculed this type of gobbledegook for years in his Dilbert comic strip and books. In fact, you can go to www.dilbert.com and find a "mission statement generator" that helps you combine an endless array of biztalk adverbs, verbs, adjectives and nouns to form nonsensical, but official sounding statements. It's funny when he does it, but the jokes on us when we encounter it in the "real" world.

If you can get His Eminence to sit still for a few minutes, try to get him to focus on a short (five words or less) brand image statement that suits your company. If you allow more than five words, it will start to sound like a mission or vision statement. The companies with the most highly developed brand images are usually associated with a single attribute:

Intel	Peformance
GE	Trust
IBM	Service
Caterpillar	Ruggedness
3M	Innovation
SAS	Business Intelligence
UPS	Reliability
New Pig	Fun
BASF	Partnering

By asking the CEO for his direction on the company's brand image, you're actually doing him a huge favor. His primary legacy will be the way the company is viewed by its various publics (customers, suppliers, employees, investors, etc.).

No one will remember, or even be vaguely aware of the many reorganizations he instituted. No one will give him much credit for the

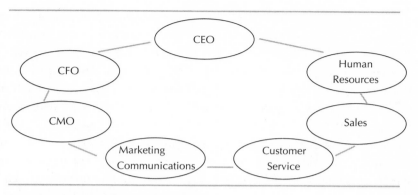

Figure 2 "Typical Branding Team Members"

inevitable downsizings and penny-pinching. And while it is important to grow the business, growing through acquisition (the most popular method these days) can get you in trouble fast.

It can also muddy an otherwise focused image. Which assumes, of course, that the CEO had a focused image in mind to begin with. Even if he has yet to seriously consider the brand image question, it's still a good idea to start him down that path. Sooner or later, you're going to need his endorsement and it's a lot better if you can reference a previous conversation on the subject.

THE CFO CONTROLS THE MONEY

The next person you need on the branding team is the CFO. This might seem like a strange choice to some, but the CFO controls the purse strings and there's no denying that branding programs can cost serious bucks.

You have to convince the CFO that branding is an *investment* that will pay significant dividends, because it is. (See Brand Equity in chapter 9.) If everybody in the company besides the CFO believes that, you're still going to have a tough row to hoe.

On the other hand, if the CFO believes in the power of branding, it really doesn't matter if you have other naysayers, because they'll climb onboard quickly once the program starts to generate results.

Ralph Oliva has put forth the startling notion that advertising practitioner success depends, in fact, on our ability to gain the support of financial managers, whether you're a client side practitioner or an agency person. He actually recommends going and talking to them about what it would take to convince them that advertising is an investment that will pay off.

What a concept! Talking to finance people about advertising is like, well, talking to advertising people about finance—it doesn't compute. But he's right. The CEO's most trusted advisor these days is the CFO. If the CFO doesn't see the need, it doesn't get done. And that includes brand image development, e-commerce initiatives, customer relationship management programs, Six Sigma and anything else with a big price tag attached.

What Oliva is really saying is that you have to show a return for the investment you're making in programs like this, and not just any measurement will do. It has to be metrics that are relevant to top management. So go ask already.

Note: Figure 10 in the Step 7 Brand Equity chapter (see page 70) offers a pretty good list of possible brand measurement metrics.

MARKETING KEEPS THE BUS ON THE RIGHT ROAD

Of course you need the involvement of the Chief Marketing Officer. That almost goes without saying, but some companies take the attitude that branding is the sole prerogative of marketing, and that is a recipe for disaster.

Marketing's primary role on the branding team is to make sure the brand position (see Step 4) is actionable and can be leveraged into a competitive advantage for the company. You have to constantly fight the vision statement thing, because people will try to force a lofty, puffed-up brand position on you that can't be implemented.

So what if you're the "world leader" or the "best place to work"? Does the market really care about that? Will your brand position repel customers or put them to sleep? It's marketing's responsibility to make sure that doesn't happen.

DON'T FORGET ABOUT INTERNAL COMMUNICATIONS

Sometimes the marketing organization includes sales, but whether it does or not, you need a sales department representative on your branding team. No group of people, except maybe the customer service department, has more customer contact and can make or break a branding program like the sales force. If they buy into the brand strategy, they'll help make it believable. If they don't, you're whistling in the dark.

My *Marketing News* colleague, Don Schultz, points out that one of the key differences between consumer products branding and B2B branding is the "people" factor. Value-added technical services, complex delivery and

Emerson spent a year preparing its employees to support its "problem solver" brand strategy with tools like this orientation program on DVD. Used with permission.

installation procedures, operator training and other people-oriented factors are much more important in business-to-business marketing situations.

"You've got to get employees and other stakeholders to support the brand promise if you're going to have any hope of success," Schultz says. "Internal marketing is critically important to the branding effort."

Emerson is an example of a company that spent over a year selling the brand strategy *internally* before it launched its program externally. Caterpillar has put more than 10,000 of its employees through branding seminars to help them understand and support the basic branding objectives. Don't overlook the importance of internal communications when you're developing a brand image program. It's essential.

MARCOM MAKES IT HAPPEN

The final members of the branding team, of course, should come from the marketing communications department and the outside brand consultants they employ. Everyone's a brand expert these days, and everyone has a "branding process," so you have to be careful which consultants you invite to join the team. But their advice and experience can make all the difference in getting the program off the ground efficiently and effectively.

It is marketing communication's job to make all the pieces fit into an integrated, consistent brand experience. No disconnects. If something is out of whack, the marcom people should be super-sensitive to this, and lobby for quick and effective change. It's not okay to take one creative approach in product advertising and another approach altogether with the annual report. The website needs to sing the same song as the tradeshow exhibits. When the sales group makes a PowerPoint presentation, it should reinforce and be consistent with your company's overall branding messages.

THE ROLE OF THE BRAND STEWARD

On one hand, you need a broadly balanced team of people to develop an effective brand image program. From the top down, and encompassing all customer touch points, this team will be charged with bringing the brand image into focus with customer expectations.

On the other hand, however, you need *one person* who is directly responsible for managing the brand image program. It's not a democracy. Decentralized organizations will have a real problem with branding, because when it comes to implementing a focused brand image, freedom of speech is unconstitutional. Like the Caterpillar brand management people advocate, say whatever you need to say, but make sure it fits your brand voice. Anything else is confusing and counterproductive.

Stewardship is about managing something important that has been entrusted to your care. The brand steward is responsible for the care and well-being of the brand. He or she should have the authority to deal with anything that threatens to weaken it.

I'm sure many b-to-b companies have yet to consider how essential it is to have a highly visible brand steward. In Texas where I live, this goes against one's basic right to "ride the open range" (don't fence me in). But barbed wire was invented for a reason, and any successful branding program has got to have a strong trail boss.

Which leads to my final point: this person's title does not have to be "brand steward." It could be brand manager, marketing manager, advertising manager or any number of other things. But it should be clearly understood in any organization who has the final say on matters related to brand management. If someone is contemplating something new for the company that will impact its image, the brand steward's expertise and advice should be solicited.

CHAPTER 3

STEP TWO

BRAND ARCHITECTURE

Brand architecture is a subject many branding experts skip, or give minimal attention to. And it's easy to understand why, because brand architecture can be boring. It's not fun like developing a brand personality or strategic like discussing brand positioning. And it's not likely to excite the C-Level execs like a thorough examination of brand equity factors will.

But brand architecture is important, nevertheless. It determines the way you organize your brand management system. And it provides guidance for adding new brands in the future. Brand architecture is like a trusty road map that only gets pulled out when you come to a fork in the road. So let's take a quick look at what you should understand about the subject.

Like most things in branding, there's no one *right* way to deal with brand architecture, nor is there any agreement on terminology. And you're probably already sensing where I stand regarding the plethora of brand words that confuse the practice and make it seem more difficult than it needs to be.

In my simplistic mind, I've narrowed the brand architecture field down to three terms: freestanding brands, overbrands and masterbrands. I'm sure the experts will snicker and flail about, but I think these three terms provide all the structure you need to navigate your way through the subject for your company or client.

Freestanding	Overbrand	Masterbrand
Synonyms:	Synonyms:	Synonyms:
Independent brand	Endorsed brand	Corporate
Stand-alone brand	Parent/Sub-brands	Company
House of brands	Family brand	
	Range brand	

Figure 3 Brand Architecture Terms

FREESTANDING BRANDS

Sometimes called "independent" or "separate" brands, this approach simply means the company has chosen to have a low profile or invisible corporate presence, and has put its image in the hands of individual product or service brands. Branding guru David Aaker, in his most recent book, *Brand Leadership* (with Erich Joachimstaler), refers to this approach as "house of brands." He devotes an entire chapter to brand architecture.

Interestingly, in his two previous books (*Managing Brand Equity* 1991 and *Building Strong Brands* 1996) both of which are considered branding classics, Aaker pays little or no attention to the subject of brand architecture. Even though he lists 21 "brand terms" in the '96 book, brand architecture is not one of them.

Another noted brand expert, Dartmouth's Kevin Lane Keller, uses the term "Brand Hierarchy" instead of brand architecture, but he takes the same basic approach in describing corporate, family and individual brands, plus brand modifiers.

Aaker cites Procter & Gamble as an example of the freestanding (house of brands) brand approach with over 80 major independent brands that make little or no connection to P&G in advertising or packaging.

A good B2B example of freestanding brands is Illinois Tool Works, a $10 billion *FORTUNE* 200 company with 47,500 employees in 200 countries. You've probably never heard of them because they let their 625 decentralized business units do the talking.

Two of those divisions, Hobart and Miller Electric, are profiled in this book as examples of branding excellence. So, at least in my opinion, you don't necessarily have to have a high corporate profile to be successful in the branding game.

OVERBRANDS

Essentially, the "overbrand" approach uses a corporate or parent brand to endorse a group of sub-brands. For example, Ford Taurus or Hewlett-Packard LaserJet.

Emerson and Cooper Industries are business-to-business marketing examples of the overbrand approach to brand architecture. In both cases, the corporate brand is used to endorse and unify a family of divisional and individual brands.

As described in the Emerson case study (see page 135), Interbrand helped Emerson managers organize sixty-six highly autonomous divisions into eight business groups, with "Emerson" being the key descriptor for each group.

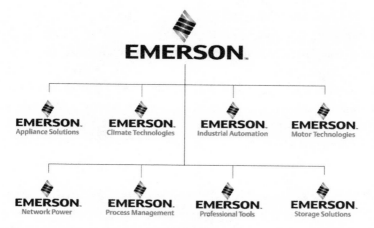

Emerson used an overbrand architecture to group sixty-six autonomous divisions divisions into eight brand platforms with "Emerson" as a key descriptor for each. Used with permission.

Similarly, Cooper's corporate identity system prominently displays the word "Cooper" for each of its electrical and tool divisions, even though several of these entities (Crouse-Hinds, Bussman, Gardner–Denver, Crescent, Lufkin, for example) have high profile images of their own.

When Cooper decided to spin-off its oilfield and industrial equipment divisions in 1995 to form a new company called Cooper Cameron, they assumed a similar approach would work for the new company. To get the new enterprise off and running, they asked their

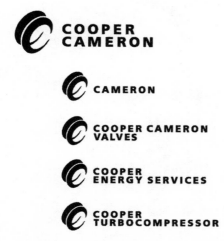

This hybrid overbrand approach for Cooper Cameron matches a distinctive "Double C" mark with the name of each division replacing the corporate name. Used with permission.

corporate identity consultants, Kass Uehling, to design a new logo featuring a dominant "Cooper Cameron" mark.

Unfortunately, the top managers at Cooper Cameron felt their customers would be more responsive to division names like Cameron, Cooper Energy Services and Cooper Turbocompressor, so they asked Kass Uehling to come up with a hybrid overbrand system that combined the names of the subsidiaries with the distinctive "Double C" mark providing the family connection (see case study on page 115).

MASTERBRANDS

The most common brand architecture system for business-to-business companies is the masterbrand approach, primarily because most B2B companies are not large enough to require a more sophisticated system, nor can they afford to properly support more than one brand.

GE Transportation

Haven't heard
we make
the world's
most powerful
jet engine?

Shhhh. We're keeping it quiet.

Thanks to an ingenious, composite front fan, the innovative GE90-115B
combines record-setting high power with remarkably low noise. You might
say it's broken a new kind of sound barrier.
To learn more, visit ge.com.

imagination at work

In General Electric's masterbrand system, the familiar GE monogram is coupled only with the advertising slogan. The division name is separated from the logo, in this case at the top of the ad. Used with permission.

Small to mid-sized industrial companies are better served putting their limited marcom dollars behind the company name and, as we will discuss in upcoming chapters, creating a brand personality for the company as a whole.

The really big B2B organizations that utilize masterbrands can afford to do anything they want. They use masterbrands because they feel they get more bang for the buck. The primary concern, however, is that one brand will adequately cover a wide range of customer expectations for a variety of product and service applications.

In the case of General Electric, it seems to work although I'm not sure how or why. The GE name and logo are placed on products as diverse as jet engines and complex medical systems, and as simple as appliances and light bulbs. When GE branched into financial, real estate and insurance services, it even seemed to work there, too.

According to former marketing communications manager Richard Costello, the reason is that GE's image has always revolved around the concept of trust. Now that new management has decided to add the extra dimension of innovation to that image (see page 141), the branding challenge becomes more complicated. Only time will tell if they can pull this off.

Another masterbrand proponent, Caterpillar (see page 97), has a somewhat simpler but difficult assignment nonetheless. In the case study, I tell how they manage their brand image with a "tone of voice" program rather than a thick binder of corporate identity do's and dont's.

MERGERS AND ACQUISITIONS

The masterbrand strategy is extremely vulnerable to corporate mergers and acquisitions. Before the merger, you have a nice, orderly brand image approach. Afterwards you have confusion or chaos.

In the case of acquisitions, the image of the acquired company will probably not fit the image of the acquiring company. But that doesn't stop well-intended people from slapping the logo of the acquirer on its vanquished properties. It's a great way to flush millions of dollars worth of brand equity down the drain.

Even when the acquiring and acquired companies are similar, you can still run into problems. For example, when Timken acquired one of its major competitors, Torrington, in 2003, the challenge was to make the two organizations act as one. Torrington was red. Timken was orange and black.

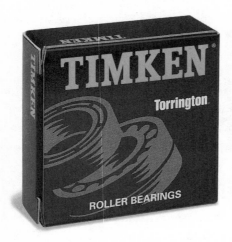

This packaging example shows the transitional strategy to use "Timken" as the master-brand and relegate "Torrington" to product brand status. Used with permission.

Fortunately, in this case, the two companies shared a common brand promise built on trust and technical competence. So the transitional strategy was to make Timken the master brand and Torrington a sub-brand or product brand. Eventually, the Torrington brand may disappear entirely based on how customers react to the interim approach.

In the case of mergers, a popular solution these days is to simply join the names of the two merging entities together to create a new name, like ExxonMobil or Fedex Kinko's. Never mind that the two company brands probably stood for very different things before the marriage.

At first glance, the joined-at-the-hip approach appears preferable to a totally new, invented name solution, but probably not for long. Eventually, the new organization has to wrestle with its own image problems and devise a branding program that will bring expectations in line with that.

As you consider the viability of a brand image development program for your company, one the first things to sort out is brand architecture. It can make everything that comes afterwards easier.

CHAPTER 4

STEP THREE

AUDIENCE IDENTIFICATION

Every company has a target audience description gathering dust in someone's file cabinet. It's possible there are as many target audience descriptions as there are marketing managers—maybe more, because these documents are routinely prepared almost every time you produce marcom projects such as brochures, ads and direct mail pieces.

I've discovered through many years of trying to work with target audience statements that most of them are not worth the paper they're printed on. (Even many of the ones I've written.) When you ask the question, "Who are we trying to reach?" all you get are clichés and superficial responses. Stock answers like "plant superintendent" or "process engineer," or "purchasing manager." If you're hoping the creative light bulbs will pop on after direction like that, good luck!

But like my grandson, Nicolas, says, "you should never give up, Papa." And embarking on a brand image development program is a good time to step back and take a fresh look at the people you need to reach with your branding messages.

EMPLOYEES COME FIRST

The first, and somewhat surprisingly, most important audience is your employees. How could employees be more important than customers? The answer is simple: if employees don't believe with all their hearts in your branding strategy, the program doesn't have a snowball's chance in hell.

Every time an outsider comes in contact with one of your employees, a chance to build or destroy your brand occurs. It doesn't matter if that employee is a highly trained sales professional or a maintenance worker who just happened to be in the wrong place at the wrong time. He or she can embody the brand personality you want, or demonstrate that it's just a figment of somebody's imagination.

It doesn't take too many bad experiences for the customer to decide it's too much hassle to deal with your company.

Interbrand's Jeffery Horn stresses the importance of doing employee research and listening carefully to their thinking about the company brand. "I have never done employee research that has not had some level of 'Ahhh-haaa!' for the leadership group," he says. "You always learn–and you send an important message–by listening and asking."

Horn points out there are dozens of ways to listen to employees through focus groups, town hall meetings, web surveys and so forth. If you assume you know the answers before you ask for their input, you're starting out entirely on the wrong foot.

This will undoubtedly come back to haunt you in later stages of a branding program. Because, as Scott Davis says in his book, *Brand Asset Management*, "the goal is to have your employees become brand ambassadors and bring the brand image, contract, and positioning to life."

After all, your brand image is the sum total of every contact your company has with customers, suppliers, investors, regulators and other audiences. If employees are delivering a different brand message than the one you intended, the greatest advertising and public relations programs in the world will be for naught.

On the other hand, if employees are acting out the brand story on a daily basis, it may not take that much advertising to spread the word around. In their recent book *The Fall Of Advertising And The Rise of PR*, Al and Laura Ries advance the controversial premise that public relations has more credibility and is more effective than advertising as a brand-building tactic.

Whether or not you agree with the Rieses about the effectiveness of advertising, it's hard to argue with their conclusion that many leading brands today have been built without it. Or very little of it. Starbucks, Krispy Kreme, LL Bean and Linux are all examples of strong brands built one customer at a time, thanks to satisfying buying experiences involving motivated, committed employees.

Scott Davis even uses the word AUDIENCE as an acronym to drive home eight things employees can do to bring a brand's positioning to life (Awareness, Understanding, Direction, Inspiration, Engagement, Naturalness, Criteria and Education see Figure 4.).

So Job One is to get the employees onboard. Flowserve, a leading Dallas-based supplier of valves, pumps and process controls that has been built largely through merger and acquisition, has dedicated more than a year of its new re-branding program to developing an internal culture that will accept and support a unified brand image.

Awareness – Every member of your internal team should be able to state your brand positioning clearly.

Understanding – Your team should fully understand why the brand positioning was chosen and how day-to-day jobs are affected by it.

Direction – Provide your team with specific service standards or behaviors to adopt so they know how to deliver on the brand positioning.

Inspiration – Show your employees clips of any research that was conducted so they can see through the eyes of your customers.

Engagement – The positioning has to be relevant to every employee in your organization. You all have to walk the talk.

Naturalness – If the right people are in place, a new positioning will soon become a natural part of their work life.

Criteria – Establish bonus criteria and MBO-like objectives, always remembering that what is not measured is not managed.

Education – Train your people to become brand ambassadors; you minimize risk and maximize positioning return by every dollar you invest.

Used with permission: From *Brand Asset Mangement: Driving Profitable Growth Through Your Brands* by Scott M. Davis

Figure 4 The A-U-D-I-E-N-C-E System   For Maximizing Employee Brand Support
Used with permission: From Brand Asset Management: Driving Profitable Growth Through Your Brands *by Scott Davis.*

UPS started with a key top management group, then worked secretly for almost a year to develop their re-branding effort, staging a series of special expos and presentations to get other managers and employees onboard before the external launch. Since virtually all SAS Institute employees are computer wizards, they used a restricted-access intranet to keep employees up to speed on their brand image program development (page 193).

Once again, there's no one right way to do it. Just make sure your employees don't find out about the new branding program through external or media sources. They'll probably reject it.

CUSTOMERS ARE NEXT

If employees are your most important branding target, then customers would certainly be next in line. An obvious place to start in prioritizing customer targets is by looking at how you segment them.

In their excellent book *Counter-Intuitive Marketing*, Kevin Clancy and Peter Krieg surmise that most B2B companies base segmentation strategies on intuition rather than hard data. For example, you target companies of a certain size (500 + employees, $100 million or more in sales, etc.), or a certain industry segment without really knowing if those are legitimate differentiators, or more importantly, if those targets are the most profitable ones.

Clancy and Krieg cite ten key factors for identifying the optimal target audience:

1. *Decision-making power*—the more responsibility a target has for making sales decisions, the more valuable it is.
2. *Sales potential*—the more a target buys or uses the product category, the more valuable it is.
3. *Growth potential*—the more a target group is growing, the more valuable it is.
4. *Lifetime value*—the more a target is expected to buy over its lifetime, the more valuable it is.
5. *Retention potential*—the more likely it is that a target can be economically sustained and therefore retained over time, the more valuable it is.
6. *Common motivations*—the more homogeneous and preemptible a target's needs are, the more valuable it is.
7. *Problem potential*—the bigger the problem the target has that the marketer can solve, the more valuable it is.
8. *Responsiveness*—the more a target group responds to a company's marketing efforts, the more valuable it is.
9. *Media exposure patterns and media costs*—the easier and less expensive it is to reach a target in media, the more valuable it is.
10. *Findability*—the more easily a target can be identified in databases, the more valuable it is.

If you haven't examined the relationships between such factors as product usage, profitability, customer retention rates and customer satisfaction levels, this might be a good time to do it. Not only will it help you write a better marketing plan, but it will also help you devise a more cohesive brand image position that will truly take your company to new levels of performance.

If you're contemplating the need to reach new markets or market segments, the first question you should ask is, "Is our existing brand image appropriate for that market?" Cessna knew its small plane image wouldn't work for business jet buyers. So they launched a new Citation division, and now they're the market leaders in both categories (see page 103). SAS didn't need a new brand to expand its image to C-Level decision makers, but they did need to refine the way they described their product offerings.

When Cameron, a large oilfield equipment manufacturer, decided to put more emphasis on aftermarket services, they created a worldwide network of "CAMSERV" service centers. The new CamServ brand successfully linked the aspects of Cameron equipment and aftermarket services in customer's minds, and helped them regain millions of dollars worth of revenues that had been lost to regional repair shops.

TARGET AUDIENCE STATEMENTS

Once you're satisfied with your market segmentation descriptions, then you can tackle the dusty old target audience statements. The more descriptive your information, the better. What turns your audience on? What turns them off? What kind of personality do they have? Are they take-charge, decisive leaders, or timid, play-it-safe bureaucrats?

The resistance you'll get in discussions of this type are predictable. "But Bob, we have all kinds of customers! We can't generalize."

And, of course, that's right. Every company has customers of every shape and color, but it's much better to have a robust, vivid picture of *one customer* in your mind than a fuzzy range of attributes that could be anybody.

In his book, *United We Brand*, Goldberg Moser O'Neill co-founder Mike Moser describes the concept of "lightning-rod targets," a term used by Boston Market to define the one person who feels passionately about the company's core brand message. The lightning-rod target is determined by his or her passion, not by how much he or she buys.

That's the customer I want my brand image program to reach, don't you?

OTHER BRANDING TARGETS

Employees and customers are the most important branding targets, but there are other audiences you should consider as you plan your brand image program. One critical group is suppliers, because supplier expectations will have a significant impact on your profitability and future success.

If the top managers of your key supplier companies *expect* that you will be more important to them in the future than you are now, they'll be willing to grant you special concessions. If they feel that your business standards are similar to theirs, they'll be more interested in forming alliances to pursue common goals. And they'll offer their unqualified endorsement when your customers bring up the subject at tradeshows and industry conferences.

And speaking of endorsements, you shouldn't overlook the roles of decision influencers like consultants, engineering firms, and industry association executives. Those people make brand-related recommendations, too.

EDITORS AND JOURNALISTS

There is a small, but highly significant group of decision influencers called editors and journalists that deserve special mention. If branding is all about defining "expectations," you better make sure that this group knows what expectations are important to you.

Early in my career, I worked for a man who had been burned by the trade press and didn't want anything to do with them. It colored my thinking for many years. But slowly and surely I came to understand that editors and journalists want the same thing you do—to get the key messages delivered to their readers. They don't want the wool pulled over their eyes. They don't want you to blow smoke at them. But if your company has embraced a certain brand position, you should make every effort to help them understand why that positioning is correct for you.

For example, if you feel you are the "advanced technology" company, then you should create a Technology Center and invite the media to tour it. You should post technology milestones on your website so they can always access it, even in the middle of the night. And each time you introduce new technology, part of your job is to compare the new improvements to older technology you hope to replace. Don't assume they can see the quantum leap forward themselves. Maybe they can, and maybe not.

ATTRACTING FUTURE EMPLOYEES

Every company wants to attract the best employees, and brand image plays a huge part in facilitating the recruitment of these individuals. Two of my step-children work for SAS Institute. One actually moved from Texas to North Carolina for the opportunity to start at the absolute bottom with that company.

He was so enthralled with their culture and reputation, he was willing to take a sizable pay cut just to get started with them. Later he talked his sister into joining the Houston office of SAS, and now she has moved to the corporate headquarters in Cary, NC.

For some strange reason, companies that have dull, stodgy brand images have dull, stodgy employees. If you want employees with a spark of enthusiasm, maybe it's time you lit a fire.

CHAPTER 5

STEP FOUR

BRAND POSITIONING

This chapter and the one that follows on Brand Personality are the most important chapters in this book. If you only grasp the concepts in these two chapters, your time reading this book will have been well spent.

In 1969, Jack Trout wrote his first article on positioning for *Industrial Marketing* magazine (later called *Business Marketing* and now *BtoB* magazine). In 1972, Trout and his partner, Al Ries, wrote a 3-part series of articles about positioning in *Advertising Age*. Finally, in 1981, their landmark book, *Positioning: The Battle For Your Mind*, was published.

It's safe to say that book changed my life, and probably a lot of other marketing practitioner lives, too. On one hand, it was a simple book: big

In 1981, Al Ries and Jack Trout turned the marketing world upside down with this landmark book. Used with permission.

type, small pages, and not too many of them. You could probably read the whole thing in an afternoon.

On the other hand, it was arguably the most significant marketing book of our era. For the first time, we were asked to examine the way people receive and store information. We were introduced to the concept of "mental ladders," and how we're not able to deal with more than seven kinds of anything at one time. Actually, in today's world of information overload, it's probably more like three or four.

IT'S ALL RELATIVE

We were taught that people see what they expect to see, and even taste what they expect to taste, regardless of the fact that our product might actually be better. Ah yes, the importance of expectations.

We were made to understand the advantages of leadership, and how futile it is for number two brands to simply act like number one brands. We were encouraged to look for "holes" in the leader's image in order to carve out a viable position for ourselves.

In fact, when you get down to it, positioning is just as much about your competition as it is about you. Much like jujitsu, you use your opponent's "weight" against them by becoming something they cannot claim.

On the other hand, if your competitor has clearly staked out a certain area, it's fruitless to try to claim that same position.

I once worked with an oilfield services company that was the third largest supplier in its category. Their two larger competitors were both waging battle over the advanced technology position. When one would make a technical claim, the other would immediately respond with a counter-claim. Back and forth they would go, with multiple ads in every issue of every leading oil industry magazine.

We advised our client to stay out of that blood bath. Instead, we quietly became the "applied technology" company, putting our emphasis on a series of training seminars to help customers learn the pluses and minuses of all the available approaches. Including ours.

POSITIONING IS THE FOUNDATION FOR BRANDING

In the Ries and Trout book, we were asked to think not only about our company's strengths, but our weaknesses as well. And how those compared to our major competitors. We were made to see that similarities and differences with competitors could be just a relevant as relationships with customers in achieving communications success.

In a way, positioning provided the basis for today's branding tidal wave by introducing the idea that you have to get inside the customer's mind in order to be successful. It's not enough to bombard people with messages, you have to help them receive that information and store it properly for future action. Like when they need to buy something.

And while this all sounds terribly obvious on the surface, I know it's not, because too many business-to-business marketing and sales managers I've dealt with over the years just don't get it. They think buying decisions are still based on features and benefits. They think customers make studied, rational selections after carefully examining all the possible options. Oh, please!

In his follow up book, *The New Positioning* (1996), Trout reminded us that more information is now being generated in a single day than the average person was exposed to in a *lifetime* two centuries ago. The English language now contains roughly a half-million words, and yet the average American is able to recognize only about 20,000 of them.

We've gone quickly from the Information Age to the "Over-Information Age." And the Internet just makes things worse, because much of the information on the web is unfiltered and unverified. The mind can't deal with it. It's overwhelming.

THE IMPORTANCE OF SIMPLICITY

So what can be done? Well, in a word: Simplify. We have to make things simple if we want to succeed in today's over-communicated world. And positioning is the key.

Positioning provides the mental hook for customers, prospects, employees, suppliers and all the other people we try to communicate with, to properly receive and store our information. It makes that information understandable and acceptable. It provides the foundation and frame of reference for what they should expect from us.

If your company is a "maverick" like Apple Computer, then thinking different is a good way to express your various product messages.

If your company is seeking to move beyond small package delivery to supply chain management expert like UPS, then asking "What can BROWN do for you?" is an inspired approach.

If your company wants to be known as the value-added partner like BASF, then reminding customers of the many ways you help make *their products* better is a very smart thing to do.

You can't be all things to all people. You can't be the mission or vision statement. The customer won't (or can't) give you credit for that much. If you try to include too many attributes in your positioning statement, it becomes mushy. The brain rejects it. You've got to keep your brand positioning simple.

WHAT POSITION IS RIGHT FOR YOU?

So how do you go about developing a good brand position? Figure 5 shows a list of possible positions that companies might occupy in a customer's mind. This is not intended to be all-inclusive. It's also not true that positions on one side of the list are necessarily the opposite of those listed on the other side.

Premium Price	+ · · + · · + · · + · · + · · +	Low Price
Advanced Technology	+ · · + · · + · · + · · + · · +	Accepted Technology
Product-Oriented	+ · · + · · + · · + · · + · · +	Service-Oriented
Product-Oriented	+ · · + · · + · · + · · + · · +	Systems-Oriented
Fun	+ · · + · · + · · + · · + · · +	Serious
Large/Resourceful	+ · · + · · + · · + · · + · · +	Small/Agile
High Quality	+ · · + · · + · · + · · + · · +	Good Value
Expected	+ · · + · · + · · + · · + · · +	Unexpected
Trusted Advice	+ · · + · · + · · + · · + · · +	New Ideas
Industry Leader	+ · · + · · + · · + · · + · · +	Up-and-coming
Generalists	+ · · + · · + · · + · · + · · +	Specialists
Craftsmen	+ · · + · · + · · + · · + · · +	Technologists
Mainstream	+ · · + · · + · · + · · + · · +	Maverick
Financially stable	+ · · + · · + · · + · · + · · +	Opportunistic
Problem-solvers	+ · · + · · + · · + · · + · · +	Self-serve

Figure 5 Positioning Grid Attributes

But in my simplistic mind, I've found it helps to give people either/or choices. If your company is known as a "generalist" then it would be rather foolish to embrace a "specialist" branding theme for one of your product lines. There probably lots of smaller specialty firms out there that are already claiming that position.

If you're large and have lots of resources, then you shouldn't worry too much about being seen as small and agile. It's like an aircraft carrier trying to call itself a PT boat. The mental picture just doesn't compute.

Everybody wants to have "advanced technology," but that's probably the most difficult position to claim and justify over the long haul. Even companies like 3M and Intel, which are known for innovation, can have dry spells. Or just as bad, they can introduce new technology before customers are ready for it, irritating them instead of delighting them.

Sometimes it's not easy embracing an appropriate brand position. I worked with a company for several years that specialized in pipeline engineering projects. Virtually everything they did related in some way to pipelines: pump stations, control systems, tank storage farms, marine unloading facilities. Their competitors were huge engineering companies that did the full gamut of engineering projects.

But when I suggested that we use "The Pipeline People" as a tagline in advertising and promotional materials, they resisted. They wanted to point out the non-pipeline assignments which accounted for less than 5% of revenues. It was all I could do to keep them focused on the 95% that was their special niche.

For another of my pipeline-related clients, Clock Spring (see case study page 109), I had to talk them out of an advanced technology position for two reasons: (1) the technology really wasn't all that revolutionary, and (2) the more it sounded like a no-brainer, the less pipeline companies would feel they had to spend several years testing it. So we went for "accepted and affordable" pipeline repair technology instead.

THE NEED FOR OUTSIDE HELP

Once you develop a short list of possible positions, then the challenge is to make it even shorter. And this is where your own judgment can get a bit cloudy, because the right answer is the one that will encourage people to do more business with you. You might not be able to discern which one that is without the objective counsel of outside experts. Your perspective is not the same as the people who might buy from you, so research is often a necessary step.

Until Fannie Mae (formerly the Federal National Mortgage Association) started working with Austin-based GSD&M, they thought they were a "quasi-governmental provider of secondary home mortgage funds." GSD&M put them in the "American dream business" helping families realize their dreams of home ownership.

If you're trying to decide between attributes like "advanced technology," "high product quality," "trustworthiness," and "system solutions," it will take some fairly sophisticated research to sort through that. But getting the right answer is critical.

YOUR BRAND POSITION MUST BE ACCEPTABLE

It's not enough to pick a brand position that's attainable, or even one that fits your long-term business objectives. You've got to make sure the positioning is acceptable to your customers and other audiences. Because brands reside in your customer's minds, they have to accept your brand position before they can give it back to you.

Monsanto found this out through a very painful foray in the uncharted waters of genetically modified foods. As described in Jonathan Low and Pam Cohen Kalafut's book, *Invisible Advantage: How Intangibles Are Driving Business Performance*, Monsanto had been pouring hundreds of millions of dollars into agricultural biotechnology in order to create a new generation of genetically modified seeds.

Farmers were big fans, enthusiastically responding to such benefits as increased nutrients, reduced spoilage and reduced chemical contamination. The company was praised for its workplace culture and for being a leader in introducing new products and business processes.

But suddenly in 2001, Italian police were seizing 120 tons of genetically engineered corn not approved by the European Union. Mobs of Brazilian protesters were breaking into Monsanto experimental farms, yanking corn and soybean crops out of the ground. At Starbuck's annual meeting, picketers were demonstrating against that company's use corn and soybean products grown from Monsanto seed. And McDonald's announced they would no longer accept Monsanto's genetically modified potatoes.

The term the media latched onto was "Frankenfoods." And despite the fact that Monsanto was following its business plan to the letter, with revenues up 28% and earnings up 5%, the stock price began a rapid decline to a new 52-week low. It lost 35% of its value within a year.

What Monsanto failed to consider was how the public would respond to its desired position as "biotechnology market leader." Or maybe the proper concern was *how quickly* the public could be expected to warm up to the concept. More than three years after the Frankenfoods fiasco, Monsanto is still trying to cultivate acceptance and approvals from their various audiences and influence groups.   .

BRAND POSITIONING VERSUS BRAND PERSONALITY

It's also important to understand the difference between brand positioning and brand personality, which we will discuss in detail in the next chapter. New Pig Corporation (see case study, page 181) did not position

To balance its fun-loving, happy-go-lucky brand personality, New Pig loads its website with dozens of technical documents and government regulations to support its spill containment industry leader position. Used with permission.

themselves as a "fun" company. That's their personality. Their position is "specialist" in spill containment products.

James Hardie, on the other hand, was getting nowhere with a "fiber cement siding products company" position. Instead, they became a company that enhances lifestyles for homeowners by making homes safer and easier to care for, and their sales of Hardiplank took off.

After many years as a trusted company that "brings good things to life," General Electric is now trying to expand its brand position to include innovation.

Cessna was known for dependable products and proven technology in prop-type small planes. Citation is now known for breaking performance barriers in business jets.

Miller Electric had a larger competitor in welding equipment that was known for making a wide variety of good quality products. Miller determined that customers wanted a supplier that could help them do better

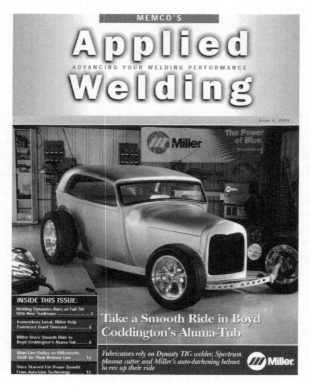

By promoting applications-oriented knowledge in printed and electronic magazines like this, Miller Electric leapfrogged its larger competitor to become number one in welding equipment. Used with permission.

welding jobs. So they became the "applications know–how" company, and now they're number one.

Hobart was the leader in food service equipment, but they had viable competitors in every product category. So they decided to leverage their unique position and become a food service *industry leader*, providing answers to questions that kept their customers awake at night.

Brand positioning is the hook that allows your audiences to receive and store information about your company's products and services. Brand personality is what you let them hang on that hook. We'll talk about that next.

CHAPTER 6
STEP FIVE

BRAND PERSONALITY

This chapter could have been titled "Brand Promise" instead of "Brand Personality". Or I could have written a separate chapter about crafting the brand promise. The problem with that is most brand promise statements are dull as dishwater, and are only understandable once you see how they're put into action.

For example, the Caterpillar brand promise is, "Caterpillar enables the world's planners and builders to turn their ideas into realities." Does that say rugged, reliable, no-nonsense, manly equipment to you? Is there any chance that customers are holding Caterpillar to that promise when they buy Cat products?

What you're held accountable for is to live up to your reputation, your image or your brand personality. In other words, if people know your personality, they expect you to act like it. On certain occasions when you don't, you generally get the benefit of the doubt. Until, of course, the disappointing behavior becomes the norm. At that point, your brand personality changes for the worse.

Now I'm not saying you shouldn't have a brand promise statement. We'll talk about that in a minute. It's just that the brand promise is (or should be) a means to an end. Ultimately the purpose of your brand is to give customers and prospective customers an *expectation* of what they should receive when they buy or specify your products and services. In that regard, it is a promise. I just wish more people would write brand promises that helped you understand what you were getting for your money.

MISSION STATEMENTS ARE NOT PERSONALITIES

There actually is a book called *The Mission Statement Book*. It was compiled by Jeffrey Abrahams and it contains 301 actual mission statements from actual companies. I'm surprised it hasn't flown off my book shelf because it's so full of hot air.

Here's an example from Diamond Shamrock:

As a cohesive team we will grow and achieve superior financial results for our company. We will consistently:

- *Focus on our customers*
- *Continuously improve everything we do*
- *Produce quality products and service*
- *Out-perform the competition*
- *Create opportunities out of change*
- *Value, respect, and develop every employee*
- *Encourage each employee's participation and ideas*
- *Be ethical, responsible, and protective of the environment*
- *Be safe, have fun, and take pride in our work*

Oops. They forgot to say they were also going to achieve world peace, balance the Federal budget and put a chicken in every pot. How careless.

Here's a much shorter one from Unisys:

We will build long-term relationships with clients, helping them creatively use information and apply technology to improve service to their customers, enhance their competitive position in the marketplace and increase their profitability.

As far as mission statements go, that one's not too bad. At least it has some probability of being acted upon by employees.

The real problem is, when I talk to companies about brand image and what customers should expect from them, they trot out the mission statement and say, "this is what we stand for."

Well, maybe in your mind, but no one else's. No customer in the world is able to relate to a mission statement when they're considering a purchase from any company. The mind just doesn't work like that. You've got to make it simpler for them.

LET PASSION PLAY A PART

As you consider mission and vision statement type values—some people call them "core values"—you should ask yourself which, if any, of these values are you passionate about?

As Mike Moser says in his book, *United We Brand*, "passion is a pretty foolproof test of whether a value is a core value." According to Moser, "Passion is what creates an emotional connection that transcends ads, public relations, brochures, or any other crafted messages that a company puts out."

He cites the Harley-Davidson logo, which is reportedly the most popular tattoo in America, as evidence of true brand passion. To a lesser extent, New Pig Corporation has generated this kind of passion among its many thousands of customers. When they get married in pig hats or make pig sounds when they call to place an order, you know you've got something special.

STAND FOR SOMETHING

The first rule in crafting a brand promise that will translate into a memorable brand personality is to stand for something. Not everything, just something.

Mission statements try to cover all the bases. You can't do that with your brand image. You've got to stand for something specific.

An easy way to get into this mindset is to think about how you would introduce a good friend to someone new. Even though you might know a lot of things about your friend, your introduction would automatically narrow it down to just one or two traits. Like, "Bill is really smart." Or "Susie is a concert pianist." Or "Fred is the most dependable guy I know."

Of course Bill, Susie and Fred have other fine qualities, but the way you get the conversation going is to talk about their intellect, piano skills, or dependability. And you branch out from there.

New Pig customers wear their pig hats and clothing on the job as well as off. Courtesy of New Pig Corporation. www.newpig.com.

Figure 6 lists some of the case history subjects described in this book, and attempts to characterize them as human personalities. See if you agree.

When you think about companies as human beings, it's easier to find words that describe attributes that will make an actual connection with your audiences.

The moment Jim Goodnight, CEO of SAS Institute (see page 193), heard the proposed slogan, "The Power To Know," he recognized instantly that was the company's brand promise. Their business intelligence software

---

If your corporate brand was a person, what kind of person would it be?

Caterpillar would be a rugged, no-nonsense, hard-working guy.

IBM would be a smart, hip, get-it-done person.

New Pig would be a fun-loving, friendly guy who's willing to try anything.

Intel would be a race car driver pushing the performance limits.

MeadWestvaco's Tango printing paper has become a tango dancer, always performing.

Miller Electric is a trusted friend, helping you master new welding applications.

Emerson is an experienced problem-solver with lots of valuable resources.

Hobart is a forward-thinking, highly intelligent leader who wants to make things better for everyone.

James Hardie is a strong protector who makes your home a safer, more comfortable place.

SAS Institute is a brilliant computer whiz who can analyze data like nobody else.

General Electric is someone you trust to come up with new ways to solve old problems.

UPS would be a super-organized, super-efficient, always reliable guy.

BASF would be a trusted partner who helps you find better ways to do things.

Figure 6   Brands as personalities

analyzes data and allows customers to "know" things they could never figure out on their own.

It's only four words, but it says precisely what they do for customers. And that makes it a great brand promise.

In a similar way, Lou Gerstner, former CEO of IBM, saw a different brand promise when he took over that company in 1993. At the time, IBM stood for mainframe computers, white-shirted technical support and irrelevant technology.

Having been an IT customer of IBM in his previous jobs, Gerstner had a different perspective. He knew customers were struggling to link hardware, software and people together to create workable, networked systems. And he knew that IBM was the most qualified company in the world to deliver on that promise.

Which brings us to the acid test for a good brand promise statement: can customers actually hold you to your so-called brand promise? If it's too unwieldy, then you need to simplify it.

CREATING THE BRAND PERSONALITY

After you have developed a brand promise that makes a connection with your audiences and stands for something you can be held accountable for, it's time to start molding and shaping that promise into a personality.

New Pig Corporation decided from day one they were going to have fun with their chosen position of spill containment products leader (of course, they weren't the leader on day one—that's just where they wanted to be).

Having fun with your brand image is not a path normally chosen by serious, play-it-safe business managers. Nine out of ten people in the same position as New Pig founders Ben Stapelfeld and Don Beaver would have named the company something safe, like "SpillCo" and printed up a tidy little product flier showing each of the products and its technical features. And off they would go to commodity land.

But the New Pig owners wanted to take a mundane, unpleasant industrial chore like sopping up machine oil leaks and turn it into something enjoyable. So they got a toll-free telephone number that spelled out H-O-T- H-O-G-S. They called their catalogs "Pigalogs." Customers were Partners In Grime (PIGs). And they gave away lots of pig hats with snouts and curly tails.

Now they have 170,000 enthusiastic, loyal customers in 40 countries who send them vacation photos from scenic mountain tops wearing pig hats.

Their brand promise is not just to deliver the world's greatest assortment of leak and spill containment products at a fair price. It's to do that and make you smile at the same time.

SLOGANS CAN TIE IT ALL TOGETHER

More than once, I've written columns in *Marketing News* critical of the widespread use of meaningless slogans. But just because most people use slogans carelessly and ineffectively, that doesn't mean they can't work for you. Here are a few tips on how to develop slogans that will actually support your branding efforts.

Good slogans remind people why they should do business with you. When you consider the personalities of real people, they remind you why you like them or don't like them and why you trust them or not. And personal nicknames, like slogans, take that a step farther. Who wouldn't want to take their car to Mr. Goodwrench for service or buy their nuts and bolts from the Ace Helpful Hardware Man?

Southwest Airlines, with its low fares and frequent flights, makes us "free to move about the country." Despite living in the heart of Southwest territory, I was for many years not a big fan. I resented being unable to get a seat assignment and having to show up at the airport an hour early in order to avoid having to sit in the middle seat.

But ultimately, they won me over. Saving money, leaving and arriving on time, and having a good choice of flight times—those are the key issues. And they do give me the freedom to move about the country at the time of my choosing and for a price I can afford. Their record as our only profitable airline in recent years is proof that a majority of travelers have responded to Southwest's basic image appeals.

Good slogans (ideally) can only be attributed to the sponsoring companies. Slogans should not be interchangeable. I pointed out in one column at least five companies were using the theme "Whatever it takes." I encouraged readers to do whatever it takes to avoid that stupidity.

This is why I like slogans such as "What can Brown do for you?" from UPS. They've taken a distinctive color that is uniquely theirs and used that as the platform for their service appeal. The color brown is a part of UPS' personality, and you can immediately tuck away any new service information about UPS in your brain's "brown folder."

More than 90% of UPS customers are able to correctly attribute the company's distinctive slogan. Used with permission.

Sometimes it's possible to incorporate your company or product name in a slogan and still satisfy the image and business requirements. Dell Computer's "Easy as Dell" is a good example of this. Now that most computer users are comfortable selecting the performance specs of their new computer online, buying a Dell really *is* easy.

It helps if your employees and customers can connect with your slogan. Most slogans are so lofty and mushy, no one can relate to them. It's like going to the opera: The fat lady is singing, but most people have no idea why or for what purpose.

When you come up with something that employees and customers connect with, it gives the program a huge boost. Like RadioShack's slogan, "You've got questions. We've got answers." You really do have questions when you walk into a Radio Shack. If you had the answers, too, you'd probably go to one of those self-serve places and just buy what you need.

St. Louis-based Emerson is a $15 billion conglomerate with a diverse array of products and services for process control, telecommunications, electronics and other markets. Its slogan, "Emerson. Consider it solved" has created the working environment for a huge organization of problem-solving zealots. It's working for them on many levels, as evidenced by fact that Emerson recently was selected by *Fortune* magazine as one of the "50 Most Admired Companies" in the world.

Like everything else in branding, there's no cookie-cutter approach to developing good slogans. It's probably one of the most demanding creative assignments we encounter. Certainly not one you'd want to leave in the hands of a rookie or amateur, so you'll probably need some top-notch creative help on this one.

BRAND SYMBOLS ARE A LOST ART

In the world of business-to-business marketing communications, the use of symbols to connote brand attributes is a lost art. Pick up any 10 trade magazines and you'll see what I mean. You can even pick up 50 if you want, but you still won't find more than a handful of symbols that help make a branding statement.

The "missing bite" from Apple Computer's apple logo helps convey the idea that you can expect something unconventional and different from them. Merrill Lynch's bull says strength to an investor audience that could probably use some added strength on any given day. And John Deere's elegant bounding deer fits nicely with their "Runs like a Deere" slogan.

The consistent use of MGM's Pink Panther character has helped Owens Corning double the insulation market share of its nearest competitor. Used with permission. Copyright 2004–2005 Owens Corning. The Pink Panther © 1964–2005 Metro Goldwyn Mayer Studios Inc. All rights reserved.

One of the most offbeat uses of symbology in business-to-business advertising is Owens Corning's adaptation of the Pink Panther character. In addition to the obvious color connection to its pink insulation product (Owens Corning was the first company to trademark a color), the panther has given the company a fun, friendly image association for almost 25 years now. And, of course, this makes it a lot easier for retailers to sell Owens Corning insulation to builders and homeowners.

In energy trade publications, you'll find the attractive, but straightforward, Shell Oil pecten. Not only does this symbol link the huge company to its humble gift shop origins, but it also helps impart an environmentally friendly image in an industry where environmentalists are constantly on the attack. Shell has upgraded its pecten at least nine times since it was first introduced in 1904, each time making it more contemporary.

In the transportation field, I always think toughness and durability when I see the bulldog symbol on the front of a Mack Truck. Apparently, this is a case of an endearing symbol being suggested by customers, because British soldiers in World War I told company representatives the blunt-nosed trucks reminded them of bulldogs as they dodged bullets and trudged through the mud in France on their way to the front with supplies.

(By the way, the Mack Truck people are not above having some fun with their beloved symbol. If you go to www.mackswimsuit.com you can vote for your favorite bulldog bathing beauty in the Bulldog Swimsuit Edition.)

Mack Trucks uses the bulldog to symbolize toughness and durability. Used with permission.

In his classic branding book, *Strategic Brand Management: Building, Measuring, and Managing Brand Equity*, Kevin Lane Keller warns against a recent trend to make brand symbols more abstract in this quest to be more contemporary. He tells the story of how Prudential Insurance had gone through 15 versions of its rock of Gibraltar symbol, finally ending up in 1983 with a stylized version that simply consisted of black and white slanting lines. Many customers couldn't see the rock anymore, so the company quickly came up with a 16th version that was modern, but more clearly recognizable.

The insurance industry is, in fact, inundated with icons. Transamerica features its prominent pyramid-shaped tower. Liberty Mutual claims the Statue of Liberty. Allstate has good hands. Mutual of Omaha displays an Indian head. Snoopy is flying overhead on the Met Life blimp. Wausau is leaving on the next train (station), and AFLAC has gone quackers for ducks.

Sadly, the most famous insurance industry symbol now belongs to a finance company. I'm talking about the red umbrella that for many

Prudential has updated the look of its Rock of Gibraltar symbol sixteen times since it was introduced in 1885. Used with permission.

years was closely associated with Travelers Insurance Co. It seems that during that company's brief stay with Citigroup, the red umbrella was abducted, and didn't go along when the insurance business was spun off again in 2002. How very strange—wouldn't it have been fun to be a fly on the wall during those conversations?

In his book, Keller talks about brand symbols as powerful ways to attract attention and enhance brand personalities by making customers like them. He mentions such prominent brand characters and symbols as the Keebler Elves, Ronald McDonald, the Jolly Green Giant and several you might not think of: Sprint's clever use of a pin dropping to promote sound transmission quality and Memorex's shattering glass to symbolize audio reproduction.

Maybe b-to-b practitioners should take a lesson from our consumer advertising brethren. Consider what Maytag has done with the lonely repairman character these last four decades: The company has become synonymous with dependability, that's what.

And look how Michelin has evolved "Bibendum," the tire-shaped boy first created in 1898. Michelin has modernized and upgraded its cuddly spokesman to transform its brand image from auto racing to friendliness and family safety.

Qantas Airways Ltd. has used kangaroos and koala bears for 50 years to symbolize the exotic attractions that might motivate people to travel halfway around the world.

Pillsbury has its Poppin' Fresh doughboy. Starkist has Charlie Tuna. Kellogg's Sugar Frosted Flakes has Tony the Tiger. Marlboro has its famous cowboy. For 40 years, Hathaway shirts had its eye-patched man.

Not only do symbols help customers remember a company's products and services, but more importantly, they help us associate positive attributes that draw us closer and make it easier for us to buy those products and services. If used properly, symbols can focus our brand expectations and shape corporate images.

Distinctive marks and symbols like these stand out in a vast, gray corporate brandscape. They are sources of pride for employees, and they help shape a company's personality to the outside world. I just can't figure out why more marketers haven't picked up on this.

DON'T BE A WALLFLOWER

The primary challenge in creating a powerful brand personality is to come up with something that differentiates your company from the pack. Of course, your brand has to connote the proper attributes that will help customers and prospects remember why they should buy from you. But too many companies are afraid to try anything bold.

I learned early in my career that bold ideas scare business managers. Only the most confident ones will select edgy concepts. But those are usually the ones that will generate the greatest results.

If you want to dance in the spotlight with the prettiest girl, you need a winning personality. Otherwise, you can sit on the sideline and watch.

Chapter 7

Step Five and a Half

Personality Makeovers

One of the hardest decisions a business manager should make is to change his or her brand personality. I've seen far too many companies switch creative approaches every time they switch marketing managers, and that's unforgivable.

We'll talk about the need for consistent execution in the next chapter, but it goes without saying, the more you change your brand personality, the less likely anyone is to understand what it is.

You can fine-tune your image advertising. Freshen it. Give it a new spin. But as long as the basic brand personality is on-target with the needs and expectations of your audiences, don't change it. Maytag has been beating the dependability drum with the Lonely Repairman since 1967 and it continues to work very well for them.

YOUR BRAND MAY BE HOLDING YOU BACK

On the other hand, your brand personality may actually be holding you back. IBM lived in Big Blue denial until it was on the brink of bankruptcy and a new CEO was hired. Deluxe was so indelibly linked to the

Even though this logo, created in 1961 by famous designer Paul Rand, had served the company well for many years, UPS wanted to move beyond the limitations of small package delivery. UPS and UPS brandmark are trademarks that are used with permission of its owner, United Parcel Service of America, Inc. All rights reserved.

dying business of check printing, its own sales representatives were starting to have self-esteem problems.

And even though you would have never known it as an outsider, UPS was struggling mightily to move beyond the limitations of small package delivery (see page 199).

Branding is not a destination, it's a journey. As you travel down the branding highway, you should constantly reassess how your brand is connecting to your various audiences and whether or not it is supporting your business objectives.

General Electric is one of our most successful companies, and when it comes to brand equity, one of the most valuable. *Business Week* estimates the 2004 brand value of GE at $44.1 billion, which is number four on the list right behind IBM, Microsoft and Coca-Cola.

But when Jack Welch handed the CEO reins to Jeff Immelt in 2001, things started to change. By the time Immelt brought Beth Comstock onboard as Chief Marketing Officer in 2003, the need for an expanded brand personality had started to coalesce.

GE was definitely one of our most trusted brands, but it wasn't getting much credit for product innovation. And in Immelt's view, innovation was going to drive GE's growth in the coming years. The brand image had to change. So out goes "We bring good things to life," and in comes "Imagination at work." See page 141 for more about that.

CHANGE FOR THE SAKE OF CHANGE

Most advertising concept changes are not for the purpose of repositioning the brand, unfortunately. The old cliché is that marketers get bored with their advertising about the time that customers are starting to respond to it. Sad, but true.

We've all seen companies that seem to introduce a new slogan every year. In the early 90s, my agency handled an oil industry division of ABB, the giant Swedish multinational. Just about the time we'd finish a new ad series or a capabilities brochure, the word would come down to stop using Slogan A and start using Slogan B. Sometimes a representative from Corporate would actually fly into town and give us a presentation on the new program. It was enough to drive you batty.

When APQC did it's B2B branding best-practices study in 2001, Cisco Systems was one of the profiled companies. Marketing representatives from Cisco waxed poetic about their tagline, "Empowering The

Internet Generation," and how it embodied the company's brand vision. The line was to be used in all communications efforts.

Three years later, they are no longer empowering the Internet generation. Now they're "The Power of The Network" or something like that. I wonder what they'll be doing three years from now. I'm sure customers will be eagerly awaiting the next big slogan change.

SPENDING MONEY TO MAKE MONEY

But there are legitimate reasons to change branding strategies, and usually this means appropriating some extra cash. UPS estimates it spent more than $20 million in 2003 alone just repainting trucks, planes and replacing uniforms and printed materials.

Launching new initiatives always costs more than maintaining the status quo, but sometimes the extra investment is necessary. If your brand personality is wrong, the sooner you set about fixing it, the sooner your image can reconnect with customers on a more appropriate level.

Unless you determine a logo and corporate identity program change to be in order, however, it might not cost any more at all. As one of my friends in the ad biz used to say, "It costs the same to run crappy ads as it does to run good ones."

What he didn't say is it always costs more to *produce* good ads, because you have to assign the work to talented people and let them spend enough time to come up with breakthrough ideas. Time is money, so yeah, it costs more.

But nobody I've ever worked with has a problem spending a little more when they see what good creative concepts can do for an image-building program. The difference is well worth the extra cost.

NEW BRANDS FOR NEW MARKETS

One of the big mistakes marketers make is trying to take a brand that has well-established meaning in one product area or industry, and put that same brand on another product in a totally different market or category.

In their book, *The 22 Immutable Laws of Branding*, Al and Laura Ries call it the Law of Expansion: The power of a brand is *inversely* proportional to its scope. In other words, the more you try to stretch a brand, the weaker it gets.

In their more recent book, *The Fall of Advertising and the Rise of PR*, Ries and Ries devote an entire chapter to the brand-building public relations opportunities that are missed when a company introduces a new product with the same brand name as an existing product.

Not only does extending a branded product line with the same name hurt press coverage, it causes confusion among customers, too. We know what to expect with Kodak film. We're not sure with Kodak digital cameras.

When Cessna decided to enter the business jets market in the late 60s, they knew the name "Cessna" wouldn't fly with the business jets crowd. That name was solidly linked with small single and twin-engine propeller planes. Entry level. Low tech.

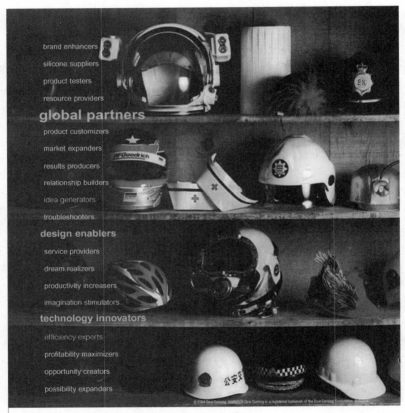

Dow Corning was able to maintain its advanced technology position by creating a "no frills" subsidiary for customers with minimal service needs. Used with permission.

So they created a new division called Citation and used their knowledge of the aviation industry to carve out a niche in business jets. Slowly over a 20 year period they proceeded to take over the whole category. Now they're the leaders in business jets *and* prop-driven small planes (see page 103). It's called having your cake and eating it, too.

COMPETING WITH YOURSELF

Dow Corning had a different problem. They had a well-deserved reputation as an innovator in silicone products, and they had lots of research and technical support people to back that up.

When low-cost foreign competitors started hammering them on price, Dow Corning created a no-frills subsidiary, Xiameter, to compete with the low-price boys. If you purchased in volume and didn't need technical service, then you could have Dow Corning quality at a greatly reduced price. From Xiameter.

General Electric uses the GE masterbrand on just about everything, from complex medical equipment to performance polymers and financial services. The exception is appliances, where GE has retained the Hotpoint brand as its entry-level product line. Hotpoint competes in the showroom with higher-priced GE Profile and GE Monogram series products.

If your brand is competing awkwardly at the lower or upper end of its price range, don't be afraid to create a new brand to protect it from that assault. The worst thing you can do is stretch your brand personality to fit all circumstances and customer needs.

Remember, the brand has to stand for something. Make sure that "something" is consistent with the personality you're aspiring to put forth.

CHAPTER 8

STEP SIX

CONSISTENT EXECUTION

It's human nature to change things. Fashions change every year. Architecture changes. Automobile styles change. And as any man can tell you, the arrangement of furniture in a house is required by some supreme law to change on a regular basis.

Unfortunately, in the world of branding, change is usually not good. The longer you stay with a branding concept, the better it will work for you. It doesn't even have to be a particularly good branding concept.

In the little lakeside community where I live, one local realtor bills herself as "the waterfront expert." I don't know that she has any more waterfront property expertise than any other realtor, but she has been

Hardy Rawls is the third actor to play the role of Maytag's Lonely Repairman since 1967. © Maytag Corporation Used with permission.

consistently using "the waterfront expert" for so many years, everybody accepts that she must be exactly that. In her newspaper ads, yard signs, literature and promotional materials, it's always the same. She is the waterfront expert.

Maytag has been using the Lonely Repairman concept to connote dependability since 1967. The original Lonely Repairman, Jesse White, actually died in 1997 and has since been replaced by two other actors, Gordon Jump and Hardy Rawls, since he retired from the position in 1988.

It doesn't really matter who plays the part of the Lonely Repairman, the important thing is that Maytag has consistently promoted the concept for more than three decades. It's easy to understand and, because it's not boastful, it's easy for consumers to accept. And now, in virtually every appliance survey, Maytag always comes out on top in dependable operation.

Kohler also started using "The Bold Look of Kohler" for its line of plumbing fixtures in the 60s, just as consumer tastes were starting to move beyond porcelain and chrome. In order to associate the Kohler name with style and leading-edge fashion, they have commissioned avant-garde photographers like David LaChapelle, Jean Claude Maillard, Hugh Kretschmer and Sacha Waldman to create a series of "As I See It" magazine ads featuring Kohler products in surreal settings. Today, when you're looking to make a bold fashion statement for your master bath, you can't go wrong with The Bold Look Of Kohler.

John Deere introduced its "Nothing runs like a Deere" slogan in 1972. State Farm insurance has also been our good neighbor since 1972. Xerox has been "The Document Company" since 1994.

LIKE A GOOD NEIGHBOR STATE FARM IS THERE.®

State Farm has been our "good neighbor" since 1972. Used with permission.

The longer you stay with a branding approach, the easier it is for customers, suppliers and other audiences to understand it and play it back to you. Most people give up on branding concepts way too soon.

IF IT'S NOT INVENTED HERE, IT SHOULD BE

It's also human nature to want to put your own stamp on advertising and marketing programs. No one wants to herd sheep, to be the passive helmsman who simply stays the course. You want to be known as the person who came up with the Big Idea, even if you only happened to walk by the room where the Big Idea was being created.

Which is better, of course, than actually trying to create the Big Idea. For some reason, managers who wouldn't profess to have a creative bone in their bodies suddenly transform into aspiring copywriters and art directors when the advertising light pops on. I'd much prefer that they simply take credit for generating creative ideas than actually insert themselves in the creative process. Taking credit is okay provided you let the great idea move forward.

IT'S NOT A DEMOCRACY

It takes a very strong, self-assured manager to resist the urge to change branding concepts. When you look at examples of companies that have stayed with winning concepts for many years, you can just imagine the pressures to change. Whining from the sales force. New campaigns launched by competitors. Management changes. Throw in a couple of your own mid-life crises, and it becomes almost too much to bear.

But branding is not a democratic process. You cannot let the majority rule (or a highly vocal minority). Someone has to take responsibility for the long-term viability of the brand. And someone has to make sure that brand messages are consistently delivered, year after year.

I'm not saying you can't freshen the approach from time-to-time. It's okay to introduce new wrinkles. Your job is certainly not to bore people to death, running the same ads every year. Just make sure the new ads fit the tone and personality that has already been established.

INSIST ON BREAKTHROUGH CREATIVE

And while we're on the subject of democracy and advertising, it's also important to point out that committee-think doesn't work either. In his very readable book, *Brand Warfare: 10 Rules For Building The Killer Brand*, David D'Alessandro says you should throw out any advertising that has been "improved" by more than three people. "The brand builder's most important job is to protect the creatives at all costs, so long as they stay true to the brand," he says.

As CEO of John Hancock Financial Services, D'Alessandro went one very surprising step further. When his agency, Hill Holliday Connors Cosmopulos, was creating the award-winning "Real Life, Real Answers" campaign, he told them to only create scenarios from their own life experiences.

The result was TV spots like the one featuring copywriter Bill Heater telling his new-born baby daughter that he just got a raise, and asking her how daddy should spend it. The final segment of this and other ads in the series was a black and white card displaying the person's name, age, income and recommended John Hancock services. Very powerful and very effective.

UNDERSTANDING YOUR TONE OF VOICE

As we discussed in Steps Four and Five, you have to *stand for something*— something that has relevance to your brand and something that can be accepted and appreciated by your audiences. But just as important as positioning and brand personality is the need to develop a consistent voice to deliver your brand messages.

Caterpillar has sent more than 10,000 employees through its basic "brand voice" seminars to help them understand the proper tone of voice. The primary purpose of these seminars is teach people who are responsible for shaping the Caterpillar brand image how to make words and images match the desired brand personality. That includes writing copy, staging photographs and preparing graphics, among other things.

You won't find a list of regulations outlawing dainty or silly Caterpillar ads. But you won't find anyone in the Caterpillar organization doing dainty or silly ads either, because those qualities are inconsistent with the Caterpillar brand voice.

In 1989, BASF embraced a TV advertising format that allowed it to feature four examples of how "We don't make a lot of the products you buy, we make a lot of the products you buy better" in each spot. Every marketing person can cite examples of TV spots that don't even communicate one product advantage, let alone four.

The format, which was also adapted for print advertising, allowed BASF marcom managers to feature products the sales force wanted to feature and still be true to the brand personality. After 15 years of consistently using this award-winning approach, the company is clearly identified with partnering and technology leadership, and did we mention it's now the world's largest chemical company?

Miller Electric surged by its larger competitor, Lincoln Electric, to take the lead in welding equipment by understanding that its tone should be the

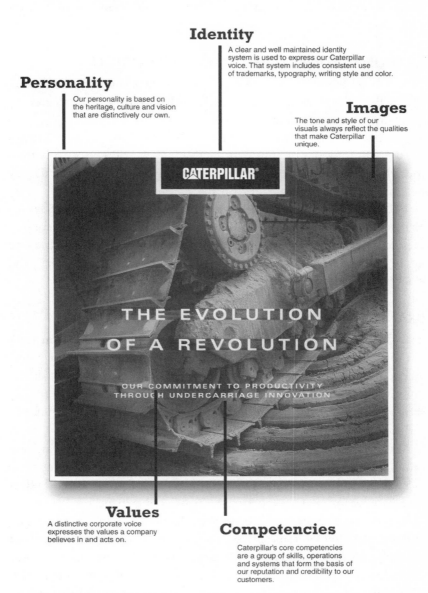

Identity
A clear and well maintained identity system is used to express our Caterpillar voice. That system includes consistent use of trademarks, typography, writing style and color.

Personality
Our personality is based on the heritage, culture and vision that are distinctively our own.

Images
The tone and style of our visuals always reflect the qualities that make Caterpillar unique.

Values
A distinctive corporate voice expresses the values a company believes in and acts on.

Competencies
Caterpillar's core competencies are a group of skills, operations and systems that form the basis of our reputation and credibility to our customers.

Instead of publishing a long list of do's and don'ts, Caterpillar uses a "tone of voice" program to maintain its image. Used with permission.

"on-site partner that helps you do better welding jobs." In their case, it's more than bold, manly copy and graphics. It's about putting the emphasis on applications-related know-how that will help customers get things done faster and better.

And hasn't IBM done an amazing job of changing its tone of voice from authoritative and arrogant to hip and helpful? Not an easy task for a behemoth.

BRANDING IS A JOURNEY, NOT A DESTINATION

Experienced brand managers know that branding is never a done deal. It may be easier to maintain an established brand image than to create a new one from scratch, but not always.

If your brand has fallen on hard times (see IBM, Deluxe), or if it stands for the wrong things in your customer's minds (see Emerson, Alberici), then the job of bringing brand expectations back into proper focus may be considerably more difficult than starting from scratch.

Just as the brand images of real people change (e.g., Martha Stewart, Arnold Schwarzenegger, Ellen DeGeneres), the brand image for companies, products and services can change, too. You have to be constantly on guard to make sure your brand doesn't lose its way among the chaos and marketplace clutter.

BRANDING TAKES NO HOLIDAY

The final point about execution of brand messages is that you can't afford to take time off. Hobart Corporation, the largest food service equipment manufacturer (see page 147), took its eye off the "industry leader" position it was in the process of claiming to run short-term promotions during an economic downturn. It paid dearly for the lapse.

Most business-to-business managers have a hard time seeing the cause-and-effect relationship between brand-building activities and profitability. If they understand anything, it's that cutting the ad budget is an easy way to make a short-term financial objective.

In the next chapter, we'll discuss the relationship between brands and building shareholder value. It's a complex and ongoing challenge, but certainly we can understand that start-and-stop communications programs are never as effective as continuous, consistently executed ones. Think of it like a conversation with a friend who's moved to a distant location. As long as you communicate frequently, all is well.

This ad lacks interest.

0%. Literally. Now if you qualify, you can get 0% financing from American Express on select Hobart foodservice equipment leased between March 1st and July 31st, 2002. At the end of your full 30 monthly payments, you'll have a $1 buyout option. And it's yours. (According to the lawyers, here's where we have to tell you that "terms and conditions apply.") Our interest in making this historic offer is simple: To help lead the foodservice industry out of one of the worst economic downturns in over a decade. And that's in all of our best interests. For the name of the participating Hobart dealer nearest you, see www.hobartcorp.com.

HOBART

Solid equipment. Sound advice.

Hobart suffered a temporary set-back in its pursuit of industry leader positioning when it switched to short-term financing promotions during an economic downturn. Used with permission.

But as soon as you stop or cut back, the person on the other end starts wondering why. Is some other market more important to you now? Have you fallen on hard times? Did you have another reorganization?

Your competition will take advantage of any hiatus to plant seeds of doubt, so don't give them the opportunity. Consistent execution is the most effective and efficient way to build brand image. It's one tool that shouldn't be left out of your branding tool kit.

As David D'Alessandro says in his *Brand Warfare:* book, "A great brand is like a bucking bronco—once you're on, don't let go." Yes, messages have to change with the times and the competition. But keep your core message constant. If you lose your grip, you'll fall.

CHAPTER 9

STEP SEVEN

BRAND EQUITY

Probably the most exasperating concept in branding has to do with placing a value on the brand assets your company employs. It's a difficult task to begin with, but made all the more troubling because branding experts are anything but agreed on how to go about it.

On one end of the spectrum, you have the super-large brand consultancies with their proprietary models and "secret sauce" formulas that only they are wise enough to apply. On the other end, you have companies and ad agencies seeking to track, on their own, one or several brand attributes that might signify brand strength improvement, but really don't tell you what the brand is worth.

WHAT IS BRAND EQUITY?

It's especially perplexing to me that branding experts can't even agree on a definition for brand equity. Most of these definitions are so stuffy and convoluted that immediately after reading them, you're not sure what point was made.

According to Jan Linderman, global director for Interbrand in the UK, brand equity and brand value are used interchangeably in the U.S. In the UK, however, they are different. "In the UK, brand equity is defined as a combination of research metrics such as awareness, knowledge, familiarity, relevance, specific image attributes, purchase consideration, preference, satisfaction, recommendation and overall brand perception or brand commitment," he says.

Brand valuation, on the other hand, is "the combination of research and financial metrics to provide a clear link between the specific marketing indicators and the financial performance of the brand." Aren't you glad I cleared that up?

A simple definition, one that anybody can follow, comes from Leo Burnett's Josh McQueen comparing brand equity to home equity. McQueen says, "Home equity is the difference between the value of the home and the value of the remaining mortgage. Brand equity is the difference between the value of the brand to the consumer and the value of the product without that branding."

At least in principle, that makes sense. But the problem is, if brand equity equals the difference between branded product sales and generic product equivalents, I guess we didn't have any brand equity before generic products became popular.

And when you really get down to it, the generic label is a brand, too. Whether it's the name of the store (or a consortium of stores) or a private label brand from a third party manufacturer, you're asking consumers to trust that brand to be a better value than the slightly higher-priced national brand.

I'm not sure there is such a thing as "products without branding." But I do agree that McQueen's definition is more right than wrong. Brand equity is all about the extra perceived value that brands represent for any product, service or company. The stronger and more focused the brand-related expectations, the higher the brand equity.

BRAND EQUITY AS A PERCENTAGE OF TOTAL WORTH

Branding pioneer Jim Gregory, CEO of CoreBrand, defines brand equity as a percentage of a company's total market capitalization that is directly attributable to its corporate brand. His firm has been tracking these values for more than a thousand companies since 1990, and he can provide both a composite numerical value as well as a dollar value for any brand in their database.

Top quintile companies in CoreBrand's "PowerBrands" ranking have more than three times the brand equity measured as a percent of total market capitalization versus mid-pack companies. The average for these companies is 15.6% brand equity as a percentage of market cap. Mid-pack companies average 4.7%. Bottom quintile companies average only 0.6%.

These top performing companies also have higher P/E ratios (stock price divided by earnings), and they receive higher financial strength ratings from financial analysts and third party observers. If you look at market capitalization as a percentage of book value of assets, the same trends appear. The top companies outperform the lesser companies by at least three to one.

So if you're truly interested in maximizing shareholder value (and who isn't?), building brand strength is one very important consideration.

Company Name	Brand Power			Brand Equity % of Market Cap
	1999	2001	2003	2003
FedEx Corp.	66.6	71.7	78.8	19.0
UPS	**77.4**	**78.0**	**18.9**	
Johnson & Johnson	68.8	73.7	77.9	18.1
Microsoft Corp.	73.6	76.0	77.3	18.3
General Electric	**67.1**	**68.8**	**75.3**	**17.2**
IBM	**60.7**	**69.2**	**72.3**	**17.1**
American Express	59.3	67.8	71.6	18.0
Hewlett-Packard	58.6	63.7	67.0	16.3
Xerox Corp.	59.3	57.0	64.0	16.6
DuPont	57.2	60.1	62.8	15.9
3M Company	46.5	53.3	62.2	14.6
Dell Computer	49.4	57.2	60.9	14.8
Intel Corporation	**56.6**	**55.4**	**59.1**	**13.7**
Apple Computer, Inc.	46.4	52.7	58.2	16.0
Sherwin-Williams	50.9	57.1	58.1	16.1
Kodak	57.1	59.6	57.8	15.1
Bausch & Lomb Inc.	50.3	53.2	57.2	15.8
Motorola, Inc.	61.3	55.2	56.6	15.0
Dow Chemical Co.	47.8	45.6	53.8	12.9
Exxon Mobil Corp.		52.8	53.5	13.6
Prudential Financial	43.1	52.8	53.2	14.3
Goodrich Company	46.1	46.2	53.0	14.7
Bristol-Myers Squibb	43.3	46.5	51.9	12.2
Honeywell	40.1	40.7	51.5	11.9
Texas Instruments	48.1	52.1	51.1	14.0
Owens Corning	**44.0**	**46.5**	**50.8**	**N/A**
Caterpillar	**48.9**	**44.8**	**50.7**	**12.4**
Goodyear Tire & Rubber	54.2	51.0	50.5	15.1
Pitney Bowes	39.2	43.4	50.2	13.5
Boeing Company	43.6	45.6	49.6	12.6
Corning Inc.	42.2	48.5	48.9	13.9
Lockheed Martin	35.2	40.1	48.7	11.8
BASF Corporation	**30.0**	**31.2**	**29.7**	**N/A**
Emerson	**23.2**	**22.3**	**23.5**	**5.8**
Deluxe Corporation	**16.0**	**12.1**	**14.4**	**2.3**

Figure 7 CoreBrand PowerBrands Rankings for Selected B2B Companies

CoreBrand arrives at these conclusions by comparing brand perceptions obtained through annual telephone research with each company's
financial data and stock performance. This is an ambitious undertaking, to
be sure. The minimum buy-in to be included in the CoreBrand database
is $100,000. That will get you an initial calibration study comparing your
brand to a small group of competitors, and a formal presentation to senior management. From that point, you pay an annual fee to have them
update the calculations and provide tracking data.

WHAT DOES THE CFO THINK?

I have suggested on numerous occasions that you should consult with
your chief financial officer about what metrics to use in tracking brand
performance. Gregory says the timing is right, because CFOs are starting to accept that brands are among a company's most valuable assets,
and they are genuinely interested in ways to quantify that value.

In his book, *Leveraging The Corporate Brand*, Gregory quotes Robert
Amen, president of Robert Amen & Associates, from a survey of 900 institutional investors in which Amen attributes about 40% of the value of
a company to tangible factors such as cash flow and earnings momentum.
He says another 20% is due to management quality and the final 40% is
based on assumptions regarding the future prospects of the industry and
that company in particular.

Whether you use the CoreBrand approach tying brand equity to
stock price/total company worth or some other method, it's still a good
idea to initiate a dialogue with your financial managers about the subject. If they haven't spent any time thinking about the contribution
brands can make to financial performance, they are most certainly not
going to support your budget requests for branding programs of any
consequence.

DO-IT-YOURSELF METHODS

Because measuring brand equity is such a difficult undertaking, I'm not
really suggesting a DIY approach is best. However, any company, no matter how small, can make some attempt to measure it. In my opinion, there's
no excuse for not trying.

David Aaker, in his book *Brand Leadership*, defines four dimensions of
brand equity: brand awareness, perceived quality, brand associations and
brand loyalty. Brand associations are slogans, symbols, product attributes
and other things a customer might connect with a brand. It's fairly easy

to see how you could put together a research questionnaire to find out how you're doing in these four areas.

Brand Awareness
Awareness often affects perceptions and even taste. People like the familiar, and ascribe good attributes to items that are familiar to them. Brand awareness is often an undervalued asset.

Perceived Quality
Influences brand associations in many contexts, has been empirically shown to affect profitability (as measured by both ROI and stock return).

Brand Associations
Anything that connects the customer to the brand. Can include user imagery, product attributes, use situations, organizational associations, brand personality and symbols.

Brand Loyalty
At the heart of any brand's value. The concept is to strengthen the size and intensity of each loyalty segment. A brand with a small but intensely loyal customer base can have significant equity.

Figure 8 Dimensions of Brand Equity   Reprinted from Brand Leadership by David A. Aaker and Erich Joachimsthaler. Used with permission.

The American Productivity & Quality Center published a *Business-to-Business Branding* best-practice report several years ago, and listed five measures of brand equity: awareness, brand image (i.e., personality), brand loyalty, perceived quality and financial measures. Those line up almost exactly with Aaker's list, with the addition of the financial metrics (e.g., sales, market share, stock price, etc.).

So if you want to track brand building progress on your own, that's a pretty good list to use. On the other hand, if you want to work with a brand valuation expert, that's okay, too. Just be prepared to shell out some bucks.

Interbrand's Linderman says all b-to-b companies can track the value of their brands. He suggests the most important metrics will be a combination of perceptual, behavioral and financial metrics (see Figure 9). Perceptual metrics measure how customers perceive the brand and their purchase intention. Behavioral metrics measure how customers actually behave towards the brand, and financial metrics measure the financial impact of customer behavior. "Brand valuation integrates all these measures into the shareholder value effect of the brand on a company's business," Linderman concludes.

Perceptual Metrics	Behavioral Metrics	Financial Metrics
Awareness	Market share	Revenue growth
Image attributes	Loyalty	Operating margin
Relevance	Lifetime value of	EVA margin
Purchase consideration	customer	Customer lifetime
Preference	Relative price	value
Satisfaction		
Recommendation		

Figure 9 Brand Value Tracking Metrics
Source: Interbrand. Used with permission

LOW COST THIRD-PARTY APPROACHES

There are plenty of branding consultants around who will walk you down the brand valuation path. And some of these will get you where you want to go for an amazingly small amount of money.

One such firm is Irvine, CA–based Trajectories Group led by Chip Shafer (see Intel Story page 159). Shafer has studied the financials of *FORTUNE 500* companies and has determined that intangibles, including brand equity, constitute as much as 70% of a company's total worth. Shafer has used these observations to develop a simple brand valuation formula:

$$B = (R + M + V) C$$

In the Shafer formula, R equals *reputation*, M equals *momentum*, V equals *vision* and C is the *connection* your brand makes with your audiences. Shafer's group uses online research and a comparative sampling of customers and prospects to gauge the strength of your brand versus one major competitor and the industry bellwether.

The final ranking produced in this exercise is a numerical value from one to one hundred. It takes about 60 days from start to finish, and the cost is less than $15,000. If this seems overly simplistic, it's that way by design. Shafer believes, and I happen to agree with him on this, that most branding consultants try to make brand valuation so complicated that only a select few geniuses can figure it out.

The reality is, unfortunately, most marketers run the other way and don't even try, or they do it once and never get around to the follow-up studies. That's a tragedy, because every company should have some measure of brand value. You know the cliché: If you can't measure it, you can't manage it. In this case, it's true.

As long as you are examining factors that your management group feels are important, there are many legitimate ways to skin this cat.

SOPHISTICATED BRAND EQUITY MODELS

FutureBrand, the consultancy that helped UPS with its gigantic re-branding effort (see page 199), uses a 4-step brand valuation process. Joanna Sedden, Executive Vice President, Worldwide Strategy, for FutureBrand walked me through the four steps.

The first step is *Segmentation*. What pieces of the business do you want to look at? Don't try to value the company as a whole even if you use a master brand architecture, because the brand will be more significant in certain segments than it is in others. You need to understand where the brand is strongest so you can leverage that strength.

The second step is *Data Collection*. Analyzing current and past financial data helps predict future growth opportunities based on different branding strategies. This is a common requirement among all brand valuation approaches, so just assume you're going to need it. Gather every kind of trend data point you can, including sales by market segment, market share by segment, profitability by segment, average sale by customer type, etc.

Scott Davis, in his book *Brand Asset Management*, lists nineteen metrics that can be used to establish a return on brand investment (see Figure 10). You can probably think of more if you put your mind to it.

The third step in the FutureBrand process is *Market Research*. They look at two key questions:

A. What is the impact of the brand on purchase decisions?

B. What percentage of purchase decisions can be attributed to the brand?

This allows you to apply a percentage to future cash flow estimates regarding the influence of brand strength.

The final step is *Competitive Benchmarking*. This phase seeks to determine the relative strength of your brand compared to major competitors. If they're stronger than you are, it may be necessary to apply a discount to your projections.

The FutureBrand process results in a dollar-amount brand value based on the brand's ability to influence future sales and profits. And if you go

1. *Brand name knowledge, awareness, recognition, recall:* measures strength of the brand as reflected by customer's ability to identify the brand under varying conditions.

2. *Positioning understanding:* identifies the level of market understanding of the positioning and selling message, by target market or segment.

3. *Contract fulfillment:* measures the degree to which your brand is upholding its brand promise.

4. *Persona recognition:* measures the degree to which your brand is consistent with its personality.

5. *Association laddering:* similar to the personality recognition metric; helps determine if your brand's value is ascending, descending or staying in place.

6. *Acquired customers:* counts customers claiming they have come to your company based on the strength of the brand.

7. *Lost customers:* counts customers claiming they have left your brand either to go to a competitive brand or because they no longer participate in the industry you serve.

8. *Market share:* looks at the percentage of potential customers (those participating in your category) that are using your brand.

9. *Current customer penetration:* estimates the amount of additional products or services you can sell to current customers based on the strength of your brand.

10. *Customer loyalty:* measures the degree to which customers continue to purchase your brand and how long the loyalty has lasted.

11. *Purchase frequency:* measures the degree to which your brand can help drive the frequency of purchases within your category.

12. *Community impact:* counts the number of positive public relations "hits" your brand gets over a given time.

13. *Brand regard:* describes how consumers feel about your brand and talk about it to others.

14. *Referral index:* determines the percentage of new business resulting from a customer, influencer, or other stakeholder recommending your brand to a potential new user.

(Continued)

15. **Customer satisfaction:** provides a "score" for customers' degree of satisfaction with your brand's product or service performance.

16. **Financial value:** reports the financial value of your brand in the marketplace.

17. **Price premium:** finds the percentage of price premium your brand is able to command over private-label brands, as well as key competitor brands.

18. **Return on advertising:** shows the financial return on advertising expenditures.

19. **Lifetime value of a customer:** total value of a customer's purchases over the relationship with your brand.

Figure 10 Brand Measurement Metrics   *Reprinted from* Brand Asset Management: Driving profitable growth through your brands *by Scott M. Davis. Used with permission.*

through the four steps periodically, you can determine if brand value is going up or down.

One practical use of this process for UPS was in regard to their acquisition of Mailboxes, Etc. UPS felt its brand wasn't very powerful at the retail level, but FutureBrand was able to show them it really was a lot stronger than the acquired company's name. Otherwise, they would never have had the guts to change it. As one FutureBrand manager said, "We helped them overcome their modesty."

BRAND SCORECARDS

Conducting brand equity research and brand valuation surveys is useless unless you can disseminate the information properly. Most manager's eyes glaze over when the lights go down during a PowerPoint presentation, especially if the presenter is a research guy. No offense, but "drone" is a word that comes to mind.

One popular way to get around this is to prepare a brand scorecard showing only your scores in the key areas. If you're testing for the five APQC brand equity metrics, show a score for each one and compare that score to several competitors. It also helps to show the previous scores (last year, six months ago, etc.).

You can index the scores so that anything over 100 is good and anything under is bad. Or you can covert your numerical scores to letters.

The problem with that is, if you start with a "C" there's only two steps higher on the ladder. It would be a serious mistake to assume if you reach the "A" level, your branding job is done. It isn't.

SAS Institute (see page 193) has experienced great success using its business intelligence software to create electronic scorecards for manager's computer screens showing key metrics changing daily as business numbers change. This approach probably hasn't been used for brand equity yet, but it's definitely plausible.

And if you link brand equity to stock price like CoreBrand does, it's an easy calculation to show brand value changing daily. It becomes a lot more interesting, however, if you devise a formula with metrics like "number of active accounts," "average purchase" or "sales of new products versus older ones." That can make your brand power scorecard truly a topic of boardroom conversation.

So you can see, there's no one right way to go about measuring brand equity. You can take the high road, the low road, or some road in between. Just make sure you do something to get your brand equity vehicle out of the garage.

It's a trip that brand managers need to make on a regular basis.

CHAPTER 10

CONCLUSIONS

I promised at the beginning of this book that I would try to make the subject of branding for business-to-business marketers easy to understand and implement. Too many so-called branding experts do just the opposite.

Hopefully, you can agree that I've done that. But as icing on the cake, here is my final attempt to summarize the entire contents of this book in just a few pages. Just like I used to carry my Arnold Palmer "How to sell" pocket cards with me in my younger days, maybe you can shrink these key points to fit a pocket-sized, laminated card and pull it out when things get confusing. Or send me $39.95 and I'll do it for you.

The Twelve Demandments of Branding

1. *Any company can do it.* Branding is not only for the very large companies. Small companies need brand power as much, if not more, than big ones. If you make a conscious decision to pursue brand-building strategies, you can do it for whatever money you were planning to spend on marcom activities. It just may take a bit longer, that's all.

2. *Start at the top.* As someone said in a recent online article, your CEO should be your chief *expectations* officer. Certainly, the CEO is your number one brand champion. He or she should have a focused understanding of the corporate brand personality and insist on reinforcing that image at every opportunity.

3. *Eliminate the silos.* Branding has to be an integrated effort with every department and subsidiary singing from the same sheet. Your annual report should convey the same brand messages as your website. Your tradeshow booth should be consistent with your trade advertising. Freedom of speech, if it means striking out on your own, cannot be tolerated in the world of branding.

4. *Get the employees onboard early.*   If they don't embrace the brand strategy, it won't work. They are living, breathing "brand ambassadors" who will convince customers, suppliers and other audiences that the brand image is real. Or not.

5. *Plan for the future of the brand.*   Make sure your brand architecture is thought through sufficiently to anticipate future expansions, acquisitions and mergers. It will be very costly to deal with this at a later stage if you don't.

6. *Know who you're talking to.*   Carefully consider the market segments that are most important to you, and do some testing to make sure the brand strategy you pursue resonates properly with them. Don't assume you can claim a brand position that doesn't fit your capabilities, or is already occupied by someone else.

7. *Keep it simple.*   Don't confuse your mission or vision statement with a focused, viable brand position. If you want customers to understand and play back your brand strategy, you have to simplify everything.

8. *Stand for something.*   You can't be everything to everybody. Pick one important attribute that will help differentiate your company from the competition, and go with that. You can introduce other attributes after your foot is in the door.

9. *Don't be invisible.*   There's no substitute for good creative. Invest in it. Take the time to do it right. Don't cut corners. And work with people who have a proven track record. Creative development is no place for rookies and amateurs. And it is definitely not a hobby for marketing managers who are bored with their jobs.

10. *Change if you have to.*   If your brand personality is saying the wrong things to your key audiences, change it. Try to keep the good parts, and add to them. Otherwise customers will be confused and think you were taken over by another company.

11. *Don't change if you don't.*   The hardest part about branding is to resist the urge to change when things are on course. The longer you stay with a branding concept, the better it will work for you. Most people give up on branding strategies way too soon.

12. *Measure your progress.*   Brands are among any company's most valuable assets. You should make every effort to quantify your brand strength and measure your progress in building and nurturing that brand.

Remember, branding is a journey not a destination. There's always something you can do to improve your brand image. However, don't get confused with the difference between minor adjustments and wholesale changes.

Your job as a "brand steward" is to manage *expectations*. When people see or hear your name, they should have a clear idea what to expect from your company. If you can get your desired brand image and customer expectations to be one in the same, you're Hall of Fame material. Call me and I'll write the next book about your branding experiences.

In the meantime, get ready for some tasty adventures down the branding superhighway led by several business-to-business marketers who have walked the walk and talked the talk. The second half of this book is twenty-one case studies, many of which have not been chronicled in any book or magazine.

Better than anything I could say or write, these stories make a compelling case for the necessity and value of B2B branding.

PART TWO
THE CASE STUDIES

CREATING PREFERENCE FOR A COMMODITY: THE ACME BRICK STORY

Some business-to-business marketing managers seem to think that a product must have significant technological advantages in order to achieve preference among consumers. Too many resign themselves to commodity status because, in their minds at least, "customers can't tell the difference."

Well, just because a customer can't articulate a product's features and benefits doesn't mean he or she can't develop a definite preference for it. Or a decided aversion to it.

Perceptual differences are often just as important as technological ones. And one company that understands this very well is Acme Brick of Fort Worth, Texas. Acme has been doing brand development work for its line of residential and commercial bricks for several decades now, and not just to its building trade audiences either. Much of what Acme does is directed to its customers' customers—homeowners and building owners.

In addition to the customary ads in architectural and construction industry trade magazines, Acme does lots of direct mail in its 7-state market area, plus a few trade shows and other things you might expect from a b-to-b marketer. What separates Acme from the building materials pack is that more than half of its $1.5 million annual budget goes into consumer media such as television ads and outdoor boards.

ENTER THE FOOTBALL STAR

The broadcast media program has grown from something even more unexpected: celebrity endorsements. In 1992, when Troy Aikman was just getting started with the Dallas Cowboys, Acme offered to furnish the brick for several Aikman family homes if he would lend his name to some modest promotional programs for Acme.

It was a handshake deal, and Acme has nurtured the relationship since that time. Now every time a home is built with Acme bricks, Acme makes a contribution to the Troy Aikman Foundation for Children.

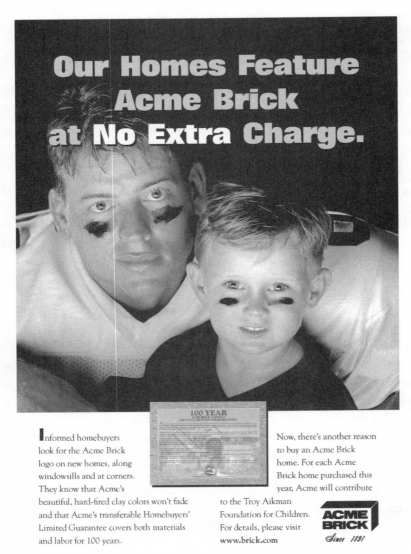

Our Homes Feature Acme Brick at No Extra Charge.

Informed homebuyers look for the Acme Brick logo on new homes, along windowsills and at corners. They know that Acme's beautiful, hard-fired clay colors won't fade and that Acme's transferable Homebuyers' Limited Guarantee covers both materials and labor for 100 years.

Now, there's another reason to buy an Acme Brick home. For each Acme Brick home purchased this year, Acme will contribute to the Troy Aikman Foundation for Children. For details, please visit www.brick.com

ACME BRICK
Since 1891

Acme has combined traditional strategies like high quality products with extended warranties and cause-related marketing featuring the Troy Aikman Foundation For Children, to build a commanding presence in its 7-state market area. Used with permission.

By 1999 more than 100 million advertising impressions about Acme's partnership with the Aikman Foundation were being made via television, billboards and point-of-sale materials.

Not only does this generate a truckload of goodwill for Acme, but it creates numerous P.R. opportunities as well. "We've found that cause-related marketing opens many avenues for us on the public relations front,"

said Bill Seidel, Acme director of marketing. In addition to reaching potential residential and commercial building customers, it also strikes a positive
chord with editors, government officials and other important audiences.

Acme has tried celebrity partnerships with other athletes, such as
former Texas Rangers slugger Juan Gonzalez. Under its "House That
Juan Built" program, Acme donated brick to build 30 homes through
Habitat for Humanity. Eller Media Outdoor Company donated dozens
of billboards in the Dallas/Ft. worth area to carry the Acme/Gonzalez
message at no charge. But Troy Aikman has been the foundation of
Acme advertising for more than a decade.

GENERATING A 10% PRICE PREMIUM

The results of these and other communication programs are easy to see.
In 1998, a telephone survey of new home buyers in four major Acme
markets revealed an 84% preference for Acme bricks. No other supplier
had more than 10% preference.

"We've become the obvious choice as far as builder company purchasing agents are concerned," said Seidel. "They're reluctant to specify
anything else." Words that would bring tears to any brand manager's eyes.

But the bottom line results are measurable, too. Seidel estimates the
Acme brand is worth an extra 10 cents for every dollar's worth of Acme
brick sold. In a typical home, this amounts to about $250 in incremental
revenue to Acme.

Put another way, you could also say that approximately $20 million of
Acme's annual $200 million brick sales is a return on the investment
that Acme makes each year in brand building. Considering their typical
$1.5 million annual budget, that's a 13-fold return on investment.

TAKING CARE OF THE BASICS

Of course Acme does a lot of other things right, too. You don't stay in
business 113 years without a firm grasp of the fundamentals. They make
high quality products and stand squarely behind them. In 1995 Acme
introduced a 100-year guarantee, which was a huge leap from the 3–5
year industry standard for most exterior building materials.

They also have aggressively promoted creative applications for brick,
including the use of brick sculpture in homes and office buildings.

And they never miss an opportunity for publicity. Just about everyone
in the Dallas/Ft. Worth area knows that Acme is the official brick of the
Dallas Cowboys. Several years ago, TIME Magazine credited Acme with

One obvious sign that a b-to-b brand has transcended its limited trade audiences is when you start to receive exposure in unexpected places. Cartoon by Drew Litton. Reprinted courtesy of the Rocky Mountain News.

the title, "Official Brick of the New Millennium" (the category was prosaic objects). And a political cartoonist in Denver once dubbed an Acme brick as the "Official Basketball of the Denver Nuggets."

On a more serious note, however, the company's involvement in worthy causes has its managers and employees popping up in newspaper stories all the time. Through the use of an outside PR specialist, Acme manages the public relations component very well.

ACME AS A PROFIT CENTER

One problem Acme hasn't figured out how to manage yet is that some builders are using the strength of the Acme brand as a profit center. It works like this: "You can buy generic, Brand X bricks for your new home for about $2,500. However, if you want the top quality Acme bricks, it will cost $3,500."

Now Acme only charges $250 more than Brand X, so the builder gets to pocket the rest. I guess that contributes to an exceptionally strong builder loyalty factor.

In Seidel's experience, there are three key benefits of building a strong brand image:

1. Better prices (Acme bricks command about 10% more).
2. Larger market share (Acme has a 50% share in its major Texas metro markets, 30–40% in other regional markets).
3. More profit to expand and improve your business.

That's the kind of vicious cycle we could all get used to: advertise aggressively, out-perform the competition, make more profit, do it again.

For managers who view advertising as an expense (vis-a-vis invest-ment), and especially those of you who view it as a discretionary expense, you might want to take another look. If someone can elevate the lowly brick to the status of "must have" product, it's time for the rest of us to get with the program. And now would be a good time to start.

Portions of this case study are reprinted with permission from *Marketing News*, November 22, 1999.

ONE STEP AT A TIME:
THE ALBERICI STORY

Most of the branding stories in this book can trace their beginning to a single event. After much discussion and deliberation, proposing and approving, someone finally made a decision to embark on a new brand image initiative. Experts were brought in to augment the in-house team. And it's usually possible for the project leaders to look back and identify a kick-off orientation meeting as the official start date.

But it doesn't have to work that way. It is possible to ease into the branding process, using your regular resources with only incremental budget increases. That's the story of how Alberici Corporation, an 85-year old construction company based in St. Louis found itself in the brand image development business. It was evolutionary, not revolutionary.

Alberici had been working with its advertising firm, Maring/Weissman since the early 90s. The agency had responded to every opportunity with handsome brochures, safety videos, websites and various collateral materials. They even designed a striking new logo and corporate identity system. But company management sensed that something more was needed.

NEW DIRECTION FROM THE TOP

New president Bob McCoole had been making lots of improvements, but customers didn't seem to understand or be aware of the changes. In fact, Alberici sales people were reporting that customers were confused about where the company was going, and whether or not it was keeping up on the latest engineering and construction technology.

If you had to describe the Alberici brand image in the late 90s, you would probably use words like old-fashioned, stodgy, inflexible and conservative. The company had a well-earned reputation for handling large and complex projects, but you probably wouldn't call them for anything under $100 million. And the company wasn't being asked to bid on projects it was really interested in bidding, like hospitals, schools and wastewater treatment plants.

So in 1999, McCoole sat down with his agency team and authorized them to start working on a new advertising program that would more accurately reflect the company's desired image. For the first time, he asked the agency to emphasize people skills rather than construction accomplishments. And he wanted Alberici to look like it was not only ready to join the twenty-first century, but lead the way.

These four ads were created to promote the passion, expertise and innovative skills of Alberici people to business leaders and construction industry targets. Used with permission.

A PASSION FOR BUILDING

Maring/Weissman responded with a series of dramatic 4-color "black and white" ads using the theme "Passion For Building." One ad featured a very serious, young black man with arms folded and the headline, "When building is your passion, each project becomes your mission." Another ad showed a hard-hatted female talking to children (also in hard hats) with the headline, "Companies that focus on the future will arrive on time."

Because the media budget was modest, Maring/Weissman decided to use business newsweeklies in three markets where Alberici had regional offices: Detroit, Atlanta and St. Louis. They also used billboards in these markets, a very unusual B2B strategy, as well as several construction industry trade magazines.

The results were immediate and significant. Opportunities to bid started coming in from unexpected sources. Employee morale soared. And Alberici's image started to undergo radical transformation.

A MID-COURSE CORRECTION

In 2001, Maring/Weissman did a qualitative research project to test the company's values against four audiences: customers, prospects, influencers (subcontractors and architects) and employees. One hundred interviews were conducted, mainly by telephone. The primary finding was that "dependability" was the attribute most closely associated with Alberici.

Customers would say things like, "You can turn your back for awhile and know Alberici is still going to get the work done. You don't have to stand over them all the time."

From this evolved the brand promise, "Unflinching Dependability." Several brochures and booklets were developed for employees to help them understand the implications of this brand promise. It was even written into the corporate identity manual.

Other key attributes from the research were: integrity, honesty, tenacity and passion. A tagline, "Bringing new and unexpected value to (insert type of project) facilities," was added to each ad and collateral piece.

The agency was careful not to lose Alberici's proud history and legacy of performance. One of the collateral pieces relates the story of company founder Gabe Alberici's decision in the 1960s to build a steel fabrication facility when a supplier failed to deliver on an important job. The project was finished ahead of schedule, and that was the beginning of Alberici's fully automated steel fabrication subsidiary, Hillsdale Fabricators.

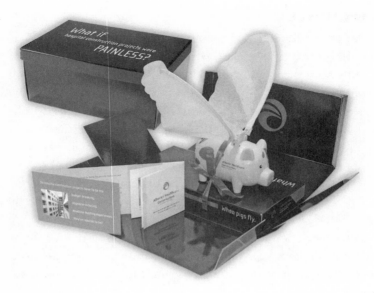

This dimensional direct mail piece urged healthcare decision makers to contact Alberici for suggestions on how to make pig-like projects fly. Used with permission–Alberici Group.

KEY MARKETS WERE EMPHASIZED

Several key markets were selected for special emphasis in 2002, and healthcare was at the top of the list. Magazine ads featuring actual Alberici employees were designed to also be used as direct mail pieces. One of my favorites featured Jim McGuirk, Carpenter General Foreman. The headline says, "My job? Staying out of your way." Copy went on to talk about how important it is for hospitals to continue to take care of patients in the midst of messy construction projects.

A 3-dimensional direct mail piece was also produced with a headline on the outside of a box that said, "What if hospital construction projects were painless?" When you opened the box, a plastic pig with expanding wings popped up, urging the recipient to contact Alberici for suggestions on how to make pig-like projects fly.

THE EARLY RESULTS

Within five months of launching the healthcare initiative, Alberici was able to trace more than $200 million in new RFPs (request for proposals) to the campaign, and $50 million in actual revenues. And much of this revenue is preliminary planning work that will lead to additional contracts later.

The company's order backlog, a key indicator of financial well-being, was up more than $400 million in 2004 versus the prior year.

But the most significant and ultimately more valuable result is that customers no longer regard Alberici as out-of-date and stuck in the 50s. Recent tracking studies now associate the Alberici brand with such desirable attributes as innovation, dependability and a passion for building.

What this proves to me is that radical brand building can be done with existing resources and modest budget increases. You don't have to re-invent the wheel. You don't even have to send it off to the wheel factory.

You just need to make sure it's properly aligned for the direction you wish to go. And if necessary, you can make adjustments on-the-fly.

USING SERVICES TO DIFFERENTIATE: THE BASF STORY

A good portion of my career has been devoted to the chemical industry, first as marketing communications manager for two Houston-based chemical manufacturers, and later as an agency consultant for a dozen other chemical-related companies. I can't think of any other industry besides the stock market where the term "commodity" comes up as much.

One reason is that chemicals are manufactured and sold to meet certain specifications. If your product is "off-spec," you're out of the game. On the other hand, anyone who can satisfy the required technical requirements is not only in the game, but considered on-par with all other qualified suppliers.

Price isn't even a differentiator, because buyers will tell you what you need to charge in order to be "competitive." Again, if you're not competitive, you're out of the game.

So how can you gain marketing leverage in an industry like that? Sometimes logistics can separate one supplier from the others—the ability to deliver or store product in ways that better serve a customer's needs, but eventually these tactics can be copied and matched by other suppliers.

SERVICES IS THE ULTIMATE DIFFERENTIATOR

A better way to differentiate is through personal services like R&D support or on-site field services. Not only are service programs harder to duplicate, but they're virtually impossible to compare on an apples-to-apples basis.

This is why becoming known as an innovative service-oriented company is the ultimate differentiating strategy, because it also connotes the *anticipation of future benefits*. If a customer thinks you are going to be more capable in a certain area, then you are. If he thinks you're more innovative, you are.

The secret, as Al Ries and Jack Trout said more than 30 years ago, is to win the battle inside the customer's mind. And that just happens to be what branding is all about.

Let's go back 15 years to 1989. BASF Ag, based in Ludwigshafen, Germany, was a second-tier chemical manufacturer with very low awareness and a fuzzy image, even though it had annual sales in North America of $3.2 billion. Most people associated BASF with magnetic recording tape because that was its most visible consumer product.

"Even though we had some very ambitious growth objectives," said Terry O'Connor, former marketing services director, "being unknown put us at a serious disadvantage against larger and better-known competitors like DuPont and Dow."

So O'Connor and his ad agency (the now defunct Geer DuBois agency) did some market research to assess the situation and lay the groundwork for a branding campaign. They identified ten attributes that could spell success over the long haul, from general associations with product quality and product diversity to more specific attributes like technical leadership and desirability as an alliance partner. They also wanted to track such factors as awareness, familiarity relative to major competitors, financial strength, efficiency and environmental responsibility.

Three possible communication strategies were developed and tested to determine which would be most effective with BASF's target audience:

> BASF Diversity
> BASF Innovation
> BASF Commitment

Innovation was the clear winner. It made the company's statements more relevant and believable, and through the enumeration of different innovative examples, it also gave the audience a sense of the diversity and breadth of BASF's product range.

WE MAKE THINGS BETTER

A long and thoughtfully different tag line was proposed by the agency for use primarily in TV ads: "We don't make a lot of the products you buy. We make a lot of the products you buy better." Another unusual touch was the use of a female announcer to deliver the line. Remember, this was at a time when booming "voice of God" narrators were standard operating procedure.

Each TV spot featured four examples where BASF products contributed to an improved end product. For example, the announcer
might say, "We don't make the carpet fiber, we make the carpet fiber
stronger."

O'Connor reports that, over the long life of this campaign, they have
been able to give promotional emphasis to virtually all the value-added
products and services the sales department wanted to emphasize and still
maintain the same, highly focused creative approach. It even survived the
closing of the original agency and shifting of responsibilities to the

*We don't make the boat, we make it
faster.*

*We don't make the safety seat, we make
it more comfortable.*

*We don't make the studio, we make it
quieter.*

*We don't make the golf clubs, we make
them more powerful.*

*We don't make a lot of the products
you buy.*

*We make a lot of the products you buy
better. BASF.*

*Each TV spot in the campaign featured four examples of how BASF helped make their
customer's products better. Used with permission.*

current firm, Cramer-Krasselt/Hempel Stefanides. Not to mention, the selling off of the magnetic tape division many years ago.

THE WORLD'S LARGEST CHEMICAL COMPANY

Today, BASF is the world's largest chemical company, with global sales of $33.8 billion and North American sales of $8 billion. In *FORTUNE* Magazine's 2003 Most Admired Global Companies, BASF is ranked number one in every chemical industry category, including "innovativeness" which used to be the sole property of DuPont.

The annual tracking studies conducted by BASF show its scores have doubled or tripled in every attribute category since the program began, while the DuPont and Dow scores have stayed the same or gone down slightly. What was once a 2-horse race is now a 3-horse race. Or you might say that BASF has re-sized the playing field to make room for a third major competitor.

"To me, the word commodity is an open admission of marketing bankruptcy," said O'Connor. "Raising the BASF profile has put us on the bid list for things people didn't know we made ten years ago, and in many cases, it gives us the inside track, because customer expectations are higher."

BECOMING SYNONYMOUS WITH PARTNERING

"We have conducted numerous customer satisfaction studies over the years, and one finding is consistently clear," adds Tony Graetzer senior vice president with BASF's ad agency, Cramer-Krasselt/Hampel Stefanides. "Companies are frequently viewed as tied on the quality of their products, but they are never viewed as tied on the quality of their services."

"On-time delivery, technical assistance, ease of ordering and other service aspects never result in tied scores," O'Connor confirms. "Here, there are clear winners, trailers and losers. Products may be at parity, but services never are. This is the area where winning companies do differentiate and can dominate."

BASF has built its brand to stand for partnership and technology leadership. By steadfastly emphasizing the way it helps make its customer's products better, the BASF image has become synonymous with partnering.

And in a market where commodity mindsets rule, you'd be hard-pressed to find anything more valuable than to be known as an innovative

MOST PEOPLE ONLY SEE A HOUSE.

WE SEE THE OPPORTUNITY
FOR ANOTHER COATINGS INNOVATION.

AT BASF, WE'RE ALWAYS LOOKING FOR WAYS TO IMPROVE COATINGS. IT'S THE REASON WE'RE
CONTINUOUSLY EXPANDING OUR ACRONAL OPTIVE® LINE OF WATERBORNE ACRYLIC RESINS. FROM
LOW VOC, TO IMPROVEMENTS IN FORMULATION COST AND PERFORMANCE, BASF IS DEVELOPING
RAW MATERIALS THAT MEET YOUR SPECIFIC NEEDS. SO IF YOU WANT THE LATEST IN COATING RAW
MATERIAL TECHNOLOGY, LOOK NO FURTHER THAN BASF. TO LEARN MORE, CALL 1-800-395-6152,
EXT. 6143 OR VISIT WWW.BASF.COM/DISPERSIONS.   **WE HELP YOU MAKE COATINGS BETTER.**

BASF

This trade ad shows how the corporate TV effort has been adapted for use with specific products and markets. The tagline here is "We help you make coatings better." Used with permission.

partner that helps make products better. That's what Brand Power is all about, and that's why BASF is No. 1 in the commodity world of industrial chemicals.

Portions of this case study are reprinted with permission from *Marketing News*, March 15, 2004.

CASE STUDY 4

Letting Your Personality Determine Your Voice: The Caterpillar Story

Most faceless, image-deprived business-to-business marketers would love to be in the position that construction-equipment giant Caterpillar was in ten years ago. But to Bonnie Briggs and her colleagues, the company's communications path was headed toward potential brand erosion and customer confusion.

Because Briggs, who formerly served as manager of corporate identity and communication for Peoria, IL-based Caterpillar Inc., knew the company's long-standing image and identity were in danger of coming apart at the seams, one stitch at a time.

"Everyone wanted to do his or her own thing," she said. "We had newly decentralized divisions creating product names by the hundreds, logo contests proliferating among employee groups, even people adding elements to the corporate logo. It was totally out of control." Especially popular were innocuous, seemingly innocent acronyms, which usually included the word CAT or Caterpillar. Unfortunately, when you put them all together, the company's primary brand asset disappeared.

"Nobody wants to play logo cop five days a week. We had to develop a way to enable thousands of Caterpillar employees to do their jobs without undermining the strength and integrity of our corporate image," Briggs said. So a decision was made to enlist the help of key people from the New York brand consulting firm Siegel & Gale. Scott Lerman, Larry Oakner, Jim Johnson, and Kenneth Cooke worked closely with Caterpillar's brand identity, communications and public affairs managers to create a program that ultimately became known as "One Voice".

DEFINING THE BRAND PERSONALITY
A lot of initial effort went into defining and focusing the Caterpillar personality and its key attributes. A list of 20 words, including such adjectives as *strong, reliable, genuine* and *serious*, was assembled to help

Caterpillar trade publication ads consistently convey the rugged, dependable attributes of the brand personality. Used with permission.

focus the mental picture people have when they think of Caterpillar. The One Voice team looked at other critical issues, too, like core competencies, primary audience needs and the company's essential business purpose.

These were not easy discussions, of course, but the team felt it was very important to capture and define that sense of oneness and voice before it was lost. They also recognized from the beginning the need to give operating level employees the freedom to exercise judgment and pursue opportunities without having to deal with a stifling manual of do's and don'ts. To do this, a three-tiered system of guidelines emerged.

The first level was called "Uniform" standards, and is the one we usually find in a corporate identity standards program: logo usage, corporate colors, type faces, package designs, and so on. These standards are considered, for the most part, inviolate and are not to be ignored or tampered with.

The second level is called "Shared/Related" standards, and includes guidelines for dealing with shared or related graphic formats like web pages, technical manuals, newsletters and product-oriented collateral materials that have a family look.

The third level is "Singular" standards, where the only guideline is making sure the communication effort fits the Caterpillar voice. This covers ads, capability brochures, direct mail, tradeshow graphics and other one-of-a-kind marcom programs. Obviously, this level is the most difficult to administer.

GETTING THE EMPLOYEES ON BOARD

To facilitate understanding and implementation of the One Voice program, and to ensure buy-in among Caterpillar employees around the world, a series of training seminars have been conducted. "Our basic seminar was originally two full days," said Briggs, "but now we offer one-day and even half-day sessions for special groups." Since the first seminar in 1994, more than 10,000 Caterpillar employees and advertising agency personnel have gone through the basic training programs.

Seminar attendees are exposed to copywriting and graphic image techniques that will help them successfully weave the Caterpillar personality into their communication efforts. For example, they study ways to achieve greater strength with photographs by cropping closer on a key aspect of the overall shot. They learn how to look for unexpected views, angles or lighting to increase drama and stopping power. They emphasize the importance of actual job site shots versus studio or plant shots. And they talk about using real employees in pictures rather than models.

In copy, the use of active verbs and strong adjectives is encouraged to convey the company personality. The need to make each sentence clear, concise, and relevant is covered, and more importantly, the need to write from the reader's point of view. Boy, don't we all wish we could put a few people through that part of the seminar!

Standards
Rules, regulations and guidelines
to prevent misuse.

Education
A range of products and
experiences tailored to the
needs of employees, suppliers,
licensees and business partners
around the world.

Resources
Links to legal requirements and online
tools for the development of new
trademarks,communication strategies
and enterprise brand
management principles.

**Public-Facing
Identity System**
Resources for dealers and business
partners to use when expressing the
Cat brand throughout the world.

Downloads
Approved trademark artwork
for internal and external use, in
print and on-line. Communication
guidelines to support consistent
language use across all media.

*On-line education modules have been developed to reinforce the learning process
and reach Caterpillar employees in remote areas. Used with permission.*

"We don't tell people to use yellow and black," Briggs said, "we just
ask them to consider which combination of words and visuals will best
demonstrate our ability to solve customer problems. When copy and
graphics don't match who we are, it simply confuses the reader."

BUILDING BRAND VALUE

When you think about it, many aspects of effective marketing communications are covered in the basic One Voice seminar. Plus, attendees learn
who they can contact for clarification or approvals in unusual situations.
The result is that Bonnie Briggs and her staff are no longer spending all
of their time as logo cops for Caterpillar's 69,000 employees.

"It's not that we don't have problems anymore," she laughed, "but
rather that thousands of people throughout the company are now aware

of what we're trying to do and how to go about it. Most of my calls now involve appropriate challenges and legitimate exceptions."

Another significant result of the One Voice program is that *Business Week* ranked the Caterpillar brand 68th in its 2004 Top 100 Global Brand Scorecard, ahead of such consumer brand power houses as Burger King, Fedex and Porsche. In conjunction with Interbrand and J.P. Morgan Chase, *Business Week* placed an asset value of $3.8 billion on the Caterpillar brand.

And largely because of the One Voice initiative, Caterpillar today has been able to maintain its master brand approach. Like many other enterprises, they learned the hard way not only do customers have trouble remembering new names, but they don't know what those names stand for. Now when legitimate reasons emerge for creating a new name, it's done so with a realistic understanding of the investment requirements and the associated risks.

The primary purpose of a brand is to build an expectation, and customers know when the name is Caterpillar, the product is likely to be durable and powerful. In the construction equipment and diesel engine business, that says a lot.

POSTSCRIPT

Since this case study was written, Bonnie Briggs retired from Caterpillar following 32 years of service. Her successor, Martin Gierke, has launched several new initiatives to expand and improve the One Voice program.

Most notable is the use of on-line education modules to reinforce the learning process and reach remote areas of the world with One Voice rationale and guidelines. Caterpillar employees can go to *www.brand. cat.com,* enter a password, and instantly access the most up-to-date branding materials available.

Gierke is also conducting new research studies to validate the Caterpillar brand message with key customer segments, and ensure its relevance. A worldwide brand council has been formed to oversee new brand strategies and drive consistency across a wide range of business activities.

Portions of this case study are reprinted with permission from *Marketing News*, July 7, 2003.

CASE STUDY 5

POSITIONING FOR THE FAST LANE:
THE CESSNA CITATION STORY

W hat would you think if Levi's introduced a new line of custom-
tailored, $2,000 tuxedos? How about a new Disney movie starring
Paris Hilton and Nicole Richie? Or a honkin' new sports car from
Hyundai?

Well that's pretty much the situation Cessna was in when it decided to enter the market for corporate jets in the late 60s. To the
general aviation industry, Cessna was a very successful and reliable
manufacturer of small, single- and twin-engine airplanes—but nothing
very sexy. The rapidly expanding business jets market, on the other
hand, was dominated by names like Lear, Lockheed, Falcon,
Commander and Hawker.

*This Cessna 150 was typical of the small, propeller-driven planes the company was
known for when it decided to enter the business jets market. Photo used with permission.*

In reality, Cessna had already built more than a thousand jet-powered airplanes. But few in the world knew this, since their only customer was the U.S. Air Force.

Even though Cessna had long enjoyed a very positive association with aviators, its image was a manufacturer of smaller, propeller-driven airplanes, primarily for flight training and personal uses. Business executives had little exposure to Cessna, unless they also happened to be pilots of light aircraft.

So while Cessna had a very good image, it just wasn't appropriate for an important new market the company wanted to enter. The only reasonable thing to do was create a new image behind a new brand name (Citation), with its own independent sales and service support organization.

UNDERSTANDING THE BUYER

In considering the market for business jets, Cessna felt its major asset was its knowledge and understanding of the psyche and behavior of aircraft owners. Ego and emotion play a significant role in this buying decision.

On the other hand, like many business-to-business marketing situations, there is a committee of customer buying influences. First, you have the "professional evaluator." This might be the company pilot or the head of its aviation department, or it might be the person they rely on for maintenance. This person is more concerned about technical details like payload, range, operating costs, etc.

The top management team, who will be among the primary users of the airplane also has a say. They're looking at things like comfort, convenience, financing, and of course, ways to rationalize the decision. Most always, the CEO is the final decision maker, but the CFO is often a big speed bump in the road. He usually can't say yes, but he can be a classic deal killer.

THE SENSIBLE POSITION

So Cessna had to consider the different motivations of all the decision makers and influencers in deciding how to crack the business jets market. Their solution was grounded in sensibility.

The initial product, the Citation I, was billed as the "sensible" choice. Even though it was slower than every other jet on the market, it could get in and out of short runways that the faster jets could not. This allowed it to take many people much closer to their desired destination.

And it was remarkably easy to fly, which was reassuring to pilots who were comfortable flying propeller planes, but worried about whether or not they could handle a jet.

The Citation I was also priced below every jet in the market, and it cost a lot less to operate. There were $580,000 turbo-props that flew 300 mph and $800,000 business jets that flew 500 mph, but nothing in between. Citation I offered 400 mph cruising for about $600,000. It filled the gap neatly and, in a word, it was the *sensible* choice.

Cessna's sensible Citation
vs.
other jets.
(Or, how to get a more versatile business plane for a lot less money.)

At right, you see a rarity. A business plane designed to be a business plane.

If *you're* in the market for a jet, scan these eight tempting reasons to own a Citation.

1. Most advanced business jet
The Citation is the first *new* business jet certified in five years. (The Grumman II was licensed in 1967, Pan Am Falcon in 1965, Learjet, BH-125, and Jet Commander in 1964, Saberliner in 1963, Lockheed Jetstar in 1961.)

So the Citation brims with latest, state-of-the-art technology. Example: the FGS-70 Flight Director in use on many 747's.

And the Citation is the *only* business jet today with the new, third-generation *high-bypass* turbofan jet engines.

2. World's most amiable jet
Pilots love the Citation because it's so simple, so safe, and such a joy to handle. There are no design-induced "no-go" items to fret about. And no need for power controls, stability augmentation devices, mach trim systems, stick pullers or pushers, or similar complexities common to other business jets. The Citation approaches the runway about 25 knots slower than its nearest competitor. Its minimum control speed on the ground is just 55 knots, compared to 102 knots for a Learjet.

Passengers love the Citation because it's so quiet and comfortable. They, too, appreciate the relaxed landing speeds. And they like the sumptuous, reclining seats. The *private* lavatory. And the luggage space—about twice that of the largest Learjet.

3. More dots on your map
The Citation has the *shortest* balanced field length of any jet—3,035 feet. This means it can fly you to rural airfields other jets can't legally and safely use.

It also means that, now and then, you'll have the satisfaction of beating owners of costlier, more

Citation: first plane to offer jet speed and the ability to slip in and out of small airfields.

pretentious jets to the same destination. Reason: your map of U.S. jetports will have 900 more dots than theirs, and you'll be able to fly *closer* to where you're going!

4. The quietest jet in the world
Latest FAA figures reveal the Citation to be the quietest jet.

Thus you'll never have to worry about expensive noise-suppression modifications.

And you'll arrive for your business appointments *unfrazzled*.

5. Costs far less to buy
The Citation is a treasurer's shortcake, for two reasons:

First, it costs anywhere from a hundred thousand or so to several *million* dollars less than other jets.

Second, it is a vastly better *buy*. By standardizing the Citation and realizing the economies of volume purchasing and quantity production, Cessna is able to furnish much more airplane for your dollar.

And the price *includes* a veritable Christmas stocking of values: aircraft, avionics, interior, training of pilots and mechanics, computerized maintenance, plus access to *factory* service centers.

6. Thriftiest jet to fly
Cruising at 35,000 feet, the fuel flow in the Citation's high-bypass engines is roughly *half* that of the next most popular jet.

The Citation's total operating cost per mile is the lowest of any jet. In fact, it's lower than that of most *turboprops* flying today!

7. Lower maintenance costs
The Citation's systems are *simpler* than those of other jets. Its fan jets are easier to service than ordinary jet engines. It is standardized—nose to tail. And it is backed by the most extensive factory service and support program in business aviation.

All this means that servicing and replacements for the Citation should go more quickly than for other jets. *So cost less.*

8. Unmatched warranty
Finally, since the Citation is sold as a complete package, the warranty *covers* a complete package. No matter what the problem, you make just one call: Cessna, the established American manufacturer that has built more airplanes than any other company in the world.

Like a 20-page brochure? Write: James B. Taylor, VP, Cessna Aircraft Co., Wichita, Kansas 67201.

cessna/CITATION SERIES 500
⊘ Member of GAMA

CIRCLE NO. 14 ON READER SERVICE PAGE

34

Cessna's first Citation ad, like its business proposition, was based on value and sensibility. Courtesy of FLYING Magazine. Used with permission.

EXPANDING THE PRODUCT LINE

"With the Citation models that followed, Cessna followed a similar strategy," said Joe Norris, Managing Partner of Citation's ad agency, Sullivan Higdon & Sink. "The company assessed the needs of the market, and then designed aircraft to satisfy those needs. So when Citation operators were ready to advance to something larger and more powerful, it was always an easy step up to the next Citation model—not a giant leap."

Now fast-forward twenty years to 1990. Citation offers nine different models and is planning the introduction of Citation X, the fastest, baddest

Even though this 1990 ad introducing the Citation X has a much more aggressive attitude, it still promotes sensible considerations like fuel-efficiency and shorter runway capabilities. © Cessna Aircraft Company. All rights reserved.

business jet in town. It travels at 92% of the speed of sound. You can eat breakfast in L.A., have lunch in New York and dinner in San Francisco.

Cessna's Citation division is now the dominant player in business jets, out-delivering all the other manufacturers combined in the markets they serve. And, just so you don't think they took their eye off the original ball, Cessna is still number one in light aircraft as well.

DELIVERING ON THE BRAND PROMISE

Is Citation still the sensible choice? Its customers think so. Because even though Citation advertising is full of emotional, testosterone stimulating words and images, it also offers logical, rational reasons why Citation represents the best combination of features and benefits for the money.

Competitors tried to ridicule the early Citation models, giving them the nickname "Slowtation." The joke was that when a Citation was struck by a bird in flight, the bird hit the airplane from the rear. You can imagine the hilarity.

But Citation management stayed the course, being very careful to deliver on the brand promise that had been made. If the planes were slower, so be it as long as they delivered more value for the money and helped customers solve more of their business travel needs.

"I'm convinced that, even though we had a great product," said Phil Michel, V.P. Marketing for Cessna, "the fact that we knew what was in the minds of our prospects allowed us to address the real issues, and effectively position our product."

STAYING IN TOUCH WITH CUSTOMERS

They never stopped surveying their customers either. Throughout that twenty-year period, Citation continually asked its customers and prospects if its products were meeting their needs. Only when they discovered a gap, did they seriously consider changing a product or adding a new model.

As Norris notes, "If Cessna had tried to introduce the Citation X back in the early 70s, the market probably wouldn't have been ready to believe they could build such an aircraft." By expanding slowly, one step at a time, they were able to evolve the product line to meet customer needs and extend the brand promise to cover a variety of products with different capabilities.

The result is a focused brand personality that promises sensible, reliable products that may not be flashy or trendy, but they get the job done nevertheless. And from the beginning, they've also promised "low risk," which says a lot for a company that had no reputation in business jets. To go from zero to market leader in twenty years is quite amazing.

And while Cessna has not established a value for the Citation brand, of the company's $3.3 billion revenues in 2002, 85% was attributable to Citation. It really shows what you can do when you set your "new brand positioning" minds to it.

MAKING YOUR BRAND SMILE: THE CLOCK SPRING STORY

When one of my best friends in business was appointed president of a small pipeline repair products company based in Long Beach, CA, he immediately called to tell me the good news and asked me to start thinking about ways to put it on the map. He knew I was intimately familiar with that market from my experiences with several other pipeline-oriented clients.

The company was named Clock Spring, which was a pretty strange name because they didn't make clocks and they didn't make springs. The founder, a somewhat eccentric inventor, was captivated by the spring-like memory of the fiberglass reinforced composite material, and since it reminded him of a clock spring, that's what he decided to call the company and the product.

THE LOW TECHNOLOGY POSITION

Even though my client was impressed by the patented technology, we ultimately decided to go in the opposite direction—to position the product not as high technology but as simple maintenance, because it was inexpensive, easy to install and easy to understand.

In the pipeline industry, "high technology" generally means expensive solutions that must be tested and evaluated over an extensive time period. And even though the Clock Spring technology had been extensively tested by the Gas Research Institute and certified by the Federal Government as an approved repair technology, we didn't want customers to get bogged down in their own evaluations. We just wanted people to use it.

With the aging pipeline network in North America and elsewhere around the world, repairing cracks and leaks was becoming an expensive and dangerous problem. You might say "a time-bomb waiting to happen" when you consider the highly explosive material inside these piping systems.

The Clock Spring sleeve, however, takes less than 25-minutes to install, does not require shutting down the pipeline, and in just a few hours, you can train your own 2-man crew to do the installation. It was also sufficiently inexpensive that you could justify using the product even if you weren't absolutely sure it was required.

The primary marketing challenge was to spread the word about Clock Spring pipeline reinforcement systems on a tiny marketing communication budget of less than $100,000. Even in the close-knit world of pipelining, that was a big challenge. We knew that placing a few straight-forward, play-it-safe product ads would hopelessly disappear in the two trade magazines we wanted to use.

GOING WAY OUTSIDE THE BOX

So we decided to go outside the box—way outside the box. To play off the quirky name, we invented a fictitious character named *Clark Spring*— Dr. Clark Spring to be precise, and we introduced Clark as a "world famous pipeline expert." With tongue firmly in cheek, we made sure that Clark appeared in every Clock Spring promotional opportunity, including magazine ads, brochures, direct mailers and tradeshow displays. The modest 10-foot tradeshow display featured a life-size cutout of Dr. Clark, complete with a waving mechanical arm.

We even produced a Christmas card with Clark hanging little spring-like ornaments on the tree. Copy below proclaimed "no-weld, no-weld," which was a joyous, holiday thought because alternative solutions required expensive and dangerous welding (as every pipeline manager knows all too well).

The one and only magazine ad we produced in 1994 was a full page, 4-color ad showing Clark pointing to a photo of the product in a simulated installation. The main headline was, "Here's the smartest pipeline repair decision you'll make all year.' Below the photo was a quote from Clark saying, "For strength, economy and convenience, my field-proven reinforcement system gets straight A's." On either side of the vertical photo were six feature/benefit callouts.

It was a fun ad, but a hard-working one, too. And it received a special award for generating the most inquiries of any ad in the leading pipeline industry trade magazine that year. We won the same award the next year, too, with a second ad emphasizing how many smart pipeline operators were already using the affordable Clock Spring repair sleeve.

The next year, to stimulate sales during the critical second quarter, we produced an over-sized mailer announcing a "60-day pipeline madness" sale. Clark was jumping for joy as he urged operations and maintenance managers to "spring into action and save."

Here's the smartest pipeline repair decision you'll make all year.

It's easy.
Each Clock Spring® kit contains everything you need for simple, *permanent* pipeline repair with no machinery required. Two man crews can be trained in just a few hours.

It's safe.
No welding or hot work is required, so Clock Spring can be safely installed while the line is fully operational.

It's inexpensive.
Clock Spring costs less and fits better than conventional steel sleeves. And it's much less expensive than pipe replacement.

It's fast.
In about two hours the repair is complete, leaving the reinforced area even stronger than when it was new.

It's proven.
The Clock Spring system has been thoroughly tested and proven reliable by respected independent research organizations under the management of the Gas Research Institute.

It's available now.
More than 8,000 Clock Spring sleeves have been installed on lines ranging from six to 56 inches. And Clock Spring offers application engineering, installation training and technical support as needed. To find out more, call 800-471-0060.

"For strength, economy and convenience, my field-proven reinforcement system gets straight A's."

PROF. CLARK SPRING, *World Famous Pipeline Expert*

©CLOCK SPRING.
Proven better, time after time.

The Clock Spring Company • 14107 Interdrive West • Houston, Texas 77032

Clock Spring is a registered trademark of NCF Industries, Inc. All rights reserved. Manufactured under license from NCF Industries, Inc.

Not only was this introductory ad for Clock Spring pipeline repair sleeves friendly and engaging, it also was the top inquiry generator in the leading trade magazine. © Robert Lamons & Associates. All rights reserved.

IT'S NOT EASY BEING SILLY

A few of the engineer-types in the company were put-off by the fun-loving Clark Spring approach. They felt it was unprofessional and silly. And when a customer would call and ask to speak to Clark, it drove them through the ceiling.

But customers did have fun with the gag, and it helped convey the idea that Clock Spring pipeline repair products were a no-brainer. Instead of getting side-tracked by the need to question, question, question and test, test, test—they simply ordered, ordered, ordered.

We created a friendly, non-threatening brand image for a small company on a limited budget, and it helped put them on the map. In my opinion, that made it worth the risk.

Typical of the quirky promotional efforts, this holiday greeting card pointed out the product's advantage of installation without welding. © Robert Lamons & Associates. All rights reserved.

The story has a sad ending, unfortunately. When my friend left Clock Spring several years later, the new managers put Clark in a closet and never let him out again. There's no telling where they might be today if they had continued the approach, but they chose to go back to fractional page ads that simply showed the product and listed its features and benefits.

The moral of the story, I guess, is that bold ideas often make people uncomfortable. But they also have the power to make customers take notice and initiate action. We not only generated lots of awareness for a previously invisible product, we also created an *expectation* of solving pipeline repair problems quickly and inexpensively.

And that, my friends, is what business-to-business branding is all about.

ARCHITECTURE FROM THE BOTTOM UP:
THE COOPER CAMERON STORY

When Cooper Industries spun off its industrial and oilfield equipment businesses in 1995, a new billion-dollar company called Cooper Cameron Corporation was created. I was involved with this enterprise from the very beginning.

Because "Cooper Cameron" was a new company headquartered in Houston with no awareness and no image, and its four divisions enjoyed solid market positions with dozens of well-known product brands, a decision was made to employ a "bottom-up" brand architecture.

The logo, designed by New York-based Kass Uehling Inc., featured a distinctive double-C monogram to suggest a precision steel component typical of the products manufactured by Cooper Cameron divisions. The bottom-up design solution combined the Double-C monogram with the names of each division, thus giving prominence to divisional names and playing on their reputations in the marketplace. See examples in the Brand Architecture chapter, page 17.

The second part of the brand architecture strategy was to allow divisions to continue the use of their many proud product names and logos. My firm spent a considerable amount of time creating style guides showing how to avoid the dreaded "dueling logos," among other things.

THE FIRST INTERACTIVE STYLE GUIDE

As a side note, our proposal included producing the usual 3-ring binder-type corporate identity manual or, for the *same money*, produce a computer-based kit with a 5 x 9 inch instruction booklet, color and logo sheets and interactive floppy discs containing templates for business cards, letterheads, envelopes and other business forms.

I was firmly convinced that 3-ring binder style guides would soon be a thing of the past, and since you first had to create a computer file in order to print anything in 1995, why not skip the printed identity manual page altogether and go directly to the digital file?

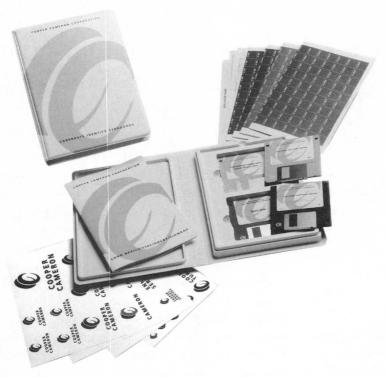

Instead of the traditional 3-ring binder, Cooper Cameron's first corporate identity manual produced in 1995 featured interactive, digital templates on floppy discs. Used with permission.

Why indeed! Because nobody had ever actually done one of those, that's why. No sooner did I get the client all excited about doing the computer-based guide, did I discover that no one we knew could tell us anything at all about how to go about producing one. And believe me, we called everyone we ever even had a casual conversation with, and some we didn't know from Adam.

But luckily we managed to stumble through without too many false steps. The bottom-up architecture didn't help, because we had two logo variations (horizontal and stacked), three color combinations and four divisions plus corporate. That adds up to a lot of templates for every form.

Plus, we also had to worry about how Cooper Cameron offices in other parts of the world would use the kit. The fear was that our templates wouldn't be compatible with foreign computer platforms, but somehow everything worked fine. Within sixty days of the new company's official launch, we had computer-based corporate identity kits produced and delivered to more than a hundred Cooper Cameron offices around the world.

CREATING THE NEW BRAND PERSONALITY

In order to start the process of building a new brand image for Cooper Cameron, we brainstormed a list of five attributes that would define the new organization and help customers understand how it would be different from the company's previous situation as a division of Cooper Industries.

The attributes were: product leadership, focused attention, aggressive marketing, responsive service and team-driven management. A pamphlet describing the core attributes was distributed to employees, along with a video for use in introducing the program in small group meetings.

And, of course, we produced an elegant, 16-page corporate brochure. Didn't think we were going to miss that opportunity, did you?

But the heart of our branding program was a trade ad campaign that ran in three leading energy industry publications. Two-page color spreads were created to expand on each of the five characteristics.

Even though the ads were produced with dark, handsome colors and bold illustrations and photos, we always injected a sense of humor in each offering. The first ad, for example, had the headline, "Cooper Cameron: The Established Market Leader (What every company hopes to achieve after the first month)."

Another ad touting the company's aggressive marketing featured a dramatic, darkly lit photo of CEO Shel Erikson sitting in a chair with the headline, "Why our customers think of us as a bunch of yes-men." (Because we won't take no for an answer.)

THE MEASURE OF TECHNOLOGY POSITION

After the first six corporate image ads had run, we continued the program for two more years with additional ads covering subjects we felt would resonate with our customers. One of my favorites addressed delivery problems that all oilfield equipment suppliers were having at that time. The headline was, "World peace, non-fattening chocolate and 100% on-time deliveries. (If we only get three wishes.)"

But after several years of producing award-winning ads that were very popular with employees and customers, ones that scored high in readership studies and played back our desired messages extremely well, I still longed for something more. Remember, this was about the time I had my GE branding epiphany, and I was looking for a way to tie all these corporate messages together under a brand positioning theme.

Jerry Lummus, head of corporate marketing for Cooper Cameron, had been pressing me to come up with something that emphasized technology and innovation. I had resisted because Cooper Cameron divisions, while all very successful in their respective markets, had little to talk about when it came to new technology. In fact, some of their so-called technology claims to fame were twenty or thirty years old.

Then it finally dawned on me. Technology is nothing more than the way things are done. A rubber band is appropriate technology to power a toy airplane because it's lightweight and cheap. I was confusing "good" technology with the need to have new, advanced technology. They're not the same at all.

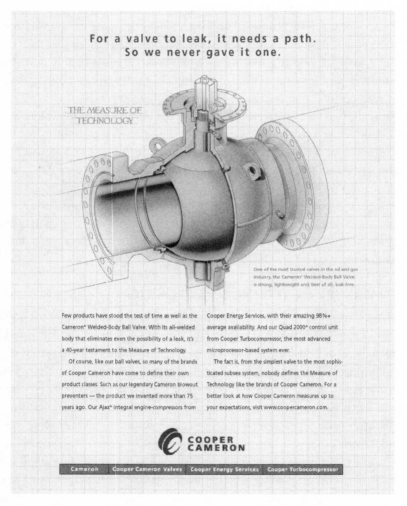

Cooper Cameron distinguished between advanced technology and technology leadership with a series of trade ads using the theme, "The Measure of Technology." Used with permission.

If more customers use your 30-year old all-welded ball valve design because it can't leak under any pressure application, then that's technology leadership. If sales were booming for your 20-year old integrated engine-compressor units because you can put them in the middle of nowhere and not worry about maintenance, then that's technology leadership.

Technology is the way things get done, and if your customers use your technology more than they use competitive technology, then guess what? You're the technology leader. You're the *measure of technology*, the yardstick by which all others are judged.

And so The Measure of Technology became the branding phrase that helped Cooper Cameron focus customer attention on its many category-leading products and services, and helped avoid the necessity of constantly justifying and defending a "new" technology position.

In fact, it actually helped us respond to untested new technology with skepticism. And in an industry that risks hundreds of millions of dollars on offshore drilling and production ventures, untested technology is definitely something that deserves a healthy dose of skepticism.

THE IRONY OF BOTTOMS-UP ARCHITECTURE

After several years, we realized that Cooper Cameron divisions were not going to do much product or brand-building advertising on their own. They didn't believe in it. They didn't feel it was necessary. And divisional manager bonuses were based on EBITDA (earnings before interest, taxes, depreciation and amortization), which means that advertising budgets just don't fit very well into that equation.

Besides, they were getting a free ride on the corporate advertising program.

The irony is that our research started to show that awareness for the corporate entity was now much higher than for any division, and since the divisions hadn't done any brand-building on their own, the only image they had was the image we had created corporately.

So what started out as a unique bottom-up brand image program ultimately became a more conventional top-down program. Which is not a problem, actually. The technology measuring stick works equally well from either end.

FROM CHECK PRINTER TO CUSTOMER EXPERIENCES: THE DELUXE STORY

Thankfully, most companies don't have to face the problems that Deluxe Financial Services was staring at in the late 90s. As the world's leading printer of checks and forms, Deluxe managers were watching the use of their core product shrink more than 4% each year.

Not only were consumers writing fewer checks, but banks and other financial institutions were merging rapidly, so there were fewer customers to call on. The total had fallen from 9,000 U.S. financial institutions (FI's) in 1997 to less than 6,000 seven years later. That's a pretty alarming decline.

Deluxe revenues would fall from over $900 million in 1997 to $700 million in 2003. But that's actually the *encouraging* news, because during that time Deluxe Financial Services (DFS), a business unit of Deluxe Corporation, was beginning to transform itself as a different kind of company, one that offered a wide variety of services to banks, savings and loans and credit unions—not just check printing.

Increasingly, checks are now viewed by financial institutions as an unfortunate requirement of a checking account. More and more people are starting to pay bills electronically, and banks have actually been encouraging them to do that.

Because banks didn't care much about selling checks, they were imposing that attitude on their customers. And there didn't appear to be any way they were going to spend much time rectifying this problem.

It was time to come up with a fresh approach. It was time to get people excited about the check-buying experience again. And it was time to show financial institutions that DFS could help them make more money and profit by actually taking over the check marketing and selling responsibility for them.

PROBING THE CHECK-BUYING EXPERIENCE

In 2001, DFS hired Copernicus Marketing Consulting to do some extensive research with end-use consumers. More than 2,000 telephone interviews were conducted. They found a tremendous gap between what consumers wanted in a printed check, and what they were actually buying. Banks were leaving a lot of money on the table by not serving that need.

"We discovered that financial institutions didn't put much effort into helping customers with their selection and purchase of checks," said Jeff VanDeVelde, Director of Marketing Strategy for DFS. "They viewed it as an unimportant and non-strategic activity, and assumed their customers did, too."

But the Copernicus research showed that consumers were a lot more interested in checks than anybody thought. And they were willing to spend more when they were made aware of better choices.

THE DELUXE SELECT PROGRAM

In early 2002, DFS developed its "on behalf" marketing program in which FI's would refer customers to DFS and DFS would interact with them to sell checks. DFS upgraded its end-use consumer

DFS staged a series of conferences featuring relationship experts like Joe Calloway to help re-position itself as a resource in enhancing customer experiences for banks and other financial institutions. Used with permission.

website and call center expertise. They also created a "voice response unit" (VRU) to handle consumer requests.

In order to create excitement for this new offering in the market, DFS staged the first of two "expos" in Chicago at the end of 2002, inviting more than 300 bankers (FI's) to attend. Noted author Geoffrey Moore (*Crossing The Chasm, Living On The Fault Line*) was the featured speaker. The basic pitch was, "outsource your check selling operation to us—we're passionate about it and we'll take better care of your customers than you will." The program was called Deluxe Select[SM], and 85 percent of attendees signed up on the spot. Eventually, 98% of expo attendees signed up for the program.

Point of sale pieces in the FI branches gave end-use customers a choice of using a toll-free 800 number or going to the DFS website where more than 100 "Customer Experience Associates" were available to help them sort through more than 70 designs and evaluate other check preferences. The objective in this phase was to get customers to think differently about DFS checks.

MORE CUSTOMER RESEARCH

In 2002, DFS commissioned Copernicus to do the largest B2B client segmentation research project ever. Four hundred eighty phone interviews were conducted with senior level bank executives, with an average 40-minute interview.

The objective was to find out more about how financial institutions perceived checks and the check selling process. What they found was that FI's were uninterested in checks, and did not view them as strategic.

Beyond check selling, the research was also designed to determine what things were important to bank executives. They observed four common objectives:

1. Generate customer satisfaction and loyalty
2. Increase revenues
3. Reduce risk and fraud
4. Improve efficiency

Many financial institutions wanted help in "creating extraordinary and compelling customer experiences." The research also probed for things that would motivate them to do more business with a partner like Deluxe.

THE DELUXE KNOWLEDGE EXCHANGE PROGRAM IS BORN

These findings led to the development of the Deluxe Knowledge Exchange program. The Knowledge Exchange series was designed to explore questions like, "What's going on in banking today?" and "How can financial institutions compete on customer experience?"

Working with Minneapolis–based Larsen Design and Martin Bastian Productions, DFS began putting together this new program to help their banking customers provide extraordinary customer experiences. It was billed as a "series for financial visionaries."

High quality quarterly magazines were mailed to DFS customers enrolled in the Deluxe Knowledge Exchange series to provide innovative ways to improve end-use customer experiences. Used with permission.

In the fall of 2003, they staged the first Knowledge Exchange conference in Boston, followed by a second one in Chicago several months later. Total attendance at the two conferences was 400 specially targeted clients. Invitees were selected based on results of the segmentation survey as persons who were most interested in improving the customer experience.

Promotion for the Knowledge Exchange program was by (1) email (60% response), (2) direct mail (additional 22% response) and the DFS sales force calling on the remainder of customers who had yet to respond. There was no print advertising.

DFS president Chuck Feltz kicked off the conference and established the tone and overall purpose. Dewitt Jones, famous photographer, director and author, spoke about celebrating what's right with life. Kevin Clancy, Copernicus Chairman/CEO provided insights from the original DFS consumer survey. Joe Calloway, branding and positioning expert, talked about creating a "Category of One."

At the conferences, a video titled "What does a model partner look like?" was showed. It featured four DFS customers talking about what they look for in a relationship with their business partners.

It was an exhilarating experience for everyone involved. Eighty percent of conference attendees signed up to be ongoing members of the Deluxe Knowledge Exchange series before they left.

THE SECOND YEAR

The 2003 programs pointed to a full-year Knowledge Exchange effort in 2004. The program has 2,800 participants representing 1,400 financial institutions, from CEOs to head tellers. Activities are divided into the four quarters of the year. A quarterly publication containing articles from leading customer experience professionals is mailed to all registered participants free of charge.

The first issue of *The Deluxe Knowledge Quarterly* focused on the importance of determining customer values. It included a welcome by Chuck Feltz and feature articles by Joe Calloway and Dewitt Jones. It also included research and in-depth articles by Kevin Clancy and strategists/authors Joe Pine and James Gilmore. And finally, it introduced the concept of a "Knowledge Exchange Collaborative."

The Deluxe Knowledge Exchange Collaborative was formed in the first quarter of 2004. It is a year-long series of four sessions at college campuses between representatives of twelve financial institutions and leading academics like Gerald Zaltman of Harvard, Len Berry of Texas A&M and Mary Jo Bittner of Arizona State.

Participants in these collaborative sessions seek to understand and improve customer experiences. Results of their efforts will be reported to all Knowledge Exchange members in the first quarter of 2005. In fact, the 2005 Knowledge Exchange series will use this insight as a foundation for further learning.

Subsequent issues of *The Deluxe Knowledge Quarterly* have focused on how to design and test purposeful customer experiences, and how to balance what customers value with what businesses value. An article by Tom Moseman (Envirosell) described strategies used by the retail industry to develop memorable customer experiences. An inspiring "Tales from the Teller Line" story told about how one bank (The RiverBank) developed its own unique customer experiences

Web seminars on "Whatever happened to targeting and positioning?" featuring Kevin Clancy and "Purposeful Experiences: Bottom line results" featuring Lou Carbone were conducted in the first two quarters of 2004.

DFS also offered audio conferences on "Nailing your Targeting and Positioning Strategy" with Kevin Clancy, and "How to interpret and manage your experience clues" with Lou Carbone in the first half of 2004. Three hundred people participated in the Carbone audio conference.

FROM TACTICAL TO STRATEGIC PARTNER

After the 2003 conferences, exit interviews showed that 97% of attendees felt the experience were excellent or good. Eighty-five percent said they would do business with DFS in the future. Eighty-seven percent viewed DFS as a strategic partner.

After the first Kevin Clancy web seminar, 85% said the content was very helpful and useful. DFS's customer retention rate is 13% better with Knowledge Exchange program participants than with non-participants.

The number of check orders for DFS is *actually up* in 2004 versus 2003, despite the drop in banking institutions and the continued trend to electronic banking.

And more importantly, banks are now asking DFS, "In what other areas can you help us improve our customer experience?" DFS has established partnerships and alliances with companies like Experience Engineering to develop programs to help financial institutions create great customer experiences.

Since many bankers now regard DFS as more of a strategic partner who they like doing business with, it has opened the door for DFS to expand its portfolio of services in growth areas not affected by the trend to electronic banking.

DFS has prepared a vision statement that says "We will not rest until we become the most trusted, most valued partner in the financial services industry—the model to which all others are judged."

And in the process of living up to that vision, they're transitioning from a provider of superior check-buying experiences to a trusted, strategic partner that helps its customers create better banking experiences. Not a bad place to be, all things considered.

COMPETING WITH YOURSELF: THE DOW CORNING STORY

Since it was established in 1943 as a joint venture between The Dow Chemical Company and Corning Glass (now Corning, Incorporated), Dow Corning Corporation has worked hard to earn a reputation as the world's most innovative supplier of silicone products. Beginning with silicone greases that made high altitude flight possible for World War II planes, to polycrystalline silicon materials for computer chips and friction-control additives for modern racecar brakes, Dow Corning has been at the leading edge of research and development for many of the breakthrough products we take for granted today.

And because silicones are such a diverse family of materials, combining the temperature and chemical resistance of glass with the versatility of plastics, the future looked very bright indeed for this well-regarded innovator. Until the late 90s that is, when small, regional competitors started taking market share away from Dow Corning by selling low-price silicone products with little or no technical support.

Hold on, they said! You can't compare Dow Corning silicones to these cheap imitators. They don't offer new product development assistance. They have no quality assurance program. They have no commitment to safety and the environment. And who knows when their deliveries will arrive?

But to some customers, those issues didn't matter. All they wanted was a lower price, and if the price was low enough, they were willing to take a chance on everything else.

RE-ACCESSING THE SITUATION

So Dow Corning managers took a deep breath and a step back to analyze what was happening. Working with their counterparts in purchasing, they quickly undertook a needs-based market segmentation study to evaluate their business model as it appealed to various types of customers. Four customer types were ultimately identified for further discussion:

Customer type	Primary needs/motivations
Standard/convenience	Off-the-shelf standard products, low-volume, transaction-driven, less long-term interest in relationships
Market-driven, low cost	High volume, many supplier sources, seeking minimum costs, minimum technical support
Strategic/partnership	High value, technology-driven, collaborative
Critical/security	Single source, collaborative

The last two groups fit the Dow Corning business model nicely, and in fact, they hadn't lost any customers fitting those descriptions. The first two groups, however, would require a new approach if they hoped to hang on to that type of customer.

Dow Corning decided to improve the match between its capabilities and the needs of the "market-driven, low cost" type of buyer. The company believed this group would probably respond to a "quality products for a reasonable price and no frills service" approach if they could devise a way to offer that profitably.

THE NO-FRILLS SOLUTION

With the booming growth of e-commerce and the comfort and convenience that business managers were starting to experience by ordering materials via the Internet, Dow Corning decided to create a no-frills, web-based business model for high-volume customers who used standard products and did not require tech support.

From a customer standpoint, this was the best of both worlds—lower prices and Dow Corning quality. And from a branding standpoint, it would allow Dow Corning to compete head-on with the low price suppliers of mature product lines, without damaging its position as a value-added leader at the premium price end of the market. (See typical Dow Corning ad touting advanced technology in the Personality Makeovers chapter, page 52.)

Once executive management made the decision to create a no-frills business model, it was full speed ahead. Landor Associates was brought in to orchestrate the brand creation process under the stewardship of Randall

Rozin, Global Manager, Branding and Marketing Communications for Dow Corning. Additional team members from Dow Corning included, the executive director for the new business model, an e-commerce manager and a marketing communications specialist.

"The Landor process was very structured and extremely stimulating," said Rozin, "and they didn't even blink when we told them we wanted the whole thing finished in 14 weeks." That meant naming the new brand, creating a logo and initial corporate identity system and designing the start-up website.

It is noteworthy that the 14-week period included the trauma of 9/11, so the branding team had to cancel several important meetings and handle decisions by long-distance. Even with those distractions, the work proceeded without a hitch.

CREATING THE NEW BRAND PERSONALITY

Using Young & Rubicam's BrandAsset® Valuator study as a guide, the group developed a list of key attributes for the new subsidiary that would resonate with the target audience. These included things like, speed/energy, trailblazing, empowering directness and honesty. Also implied were "quality" and "reliability" because of the Dow Corning pedigree.

A key word that surfaced during this time was "diameter." A diameter goes directly through a circle, bisecting it, just as Dow Corning was bisecting its own business with the new web-based business model. It also contains the word part "meter" which connotes measurement and setting standards.

Altogether, more than 2,500 possible names were considered. Of these, 151 were put through a preliminary legal search and eighteen were given a full legal search and native language check to ensure against negative connotations.

The new measure of value.
From Dow Corning.

|XIAMETER|®

With the help of an outside consultant, Landor Associates, Dow Corning chose an entirely new word for its "no frills" web-based business. © Dow Corning. Used with permission.

The winner was an entirely new word, XIAMETER, which is pronounced with a "z" like xylophone. A tagline, "The new measure of value from Dow Corning" was immediately added to clarify the brand promise and make the parent company connection.

"We sought to create a name we could own. Initially, when we put Xiameter in an Internet search engine like Google, there were zero hits," said Rozin. "Now you can do the same thing and get over 78,000 associations."

AN UNQUALIFIED BUSINESS SUCCESS

The Xiameter website went live in March, 2002. It offered more than 300 silicon-based fluids, resins and adhesive/sealants for shipment to 50 destination countries. Once a customer went through a simple registration process, he or she could get pricing and minimum/maximum product quantities, determine payment terms and receive guaranteed shipping dates. Customers could also access product safety information and download certificates of chemical equivalencies.

Dow Corning does not report sales for Xiameter independently. However, there has been a significant increase in overall company sales and profitability since Xiameter was created. The actual numbers are as follows:

Year	Total Sales	Net Income
2001	$2.44 billion	$ 36.3 million
2002	$2.61 billion	$141.6 million
2003	$2.87 billion	$177.0 million
2004	$3.37 billion	$288.8 million

Monthly Xiameter transactions have grown continuously since its inception. And acceptance of Xiameter outside of the United States has been much greater than anticipated, especially in high-growth potential countries like China. The number of authorized ship-to destinations has now been expanded to 82 countries.

Rozin says the cannibalization of Dow Corning sales by Xiameter has been very low—much less than forecast.

AN UNQUALIFIED BRANDING SUCCESS

But the most significant result has been the re-vitalization of the Dow Corning brand. "By addressing customer needs at various levels of segmentation, including the lower price points via the Xiameter®

brand, we've been able to put a more focused effort into building the value-added, leading innovator image for Dow Corning." Rozin said.

This image helps Dow Corning form closer strategic relationships with key customers, and encourages other prospective clients to approach Dow Corning with developmental opportunities. And it has had a noticeable effect on morale among the company's many "whiz-bang scientists." The best scientists, after all, want to work for the best science company.

"Before Xiameter," Rozin concluded, "you rarely heard the word 'brand' at Dow Corning. Now it's an important corporate priority. We realize how critical it is to help create a positive branding experience for our customer across the hundreds of daily touchpoints between our company and theirs."

Amazing what a little competition can do for the soul, and for the bottom line.

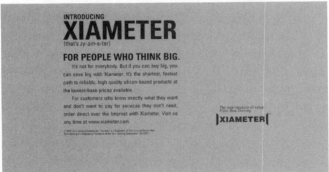

This trade magazine ad is typical of several that were developed to introduce the on-line Xiameter subsidiary. © Dow Corning. Used with permission.

Portions of this case study are reprinted with permission from *Marketing News*, June 15, 2005.

ADDING PIECES TO MORE THAN THE WHOLE: THE EMERSON STORY

Here's a fun riddle: What do you get when you combine some plumbing tools with an electric motor, a telecommunications system and a garbage disposal? And while you're at it, you might as well toss in a closet storage kit, some process control valves and an air conditioning thermostat. Oh yeah, and a refrigeration compressor, a dishwasher motor and some asset management software.

Back in the 70s we would've called that a conglomerate, but that's not a very popular term these days. No, and it's not the best way to build shareholder value either.

Even though St. Louis-based Emerson Electric had enjoyed 43 consecutive years of increased earnings per share (1956 to 2000) and 44 consecutive years of increased dividends, they knew the technology leadership of their 60-plus divisions was not being transferred to the parent company. Stated another way, they knew that brand contribution to company earnings was sub-par.

The company had a reputation as a maker of components (albeit, very good components) and that was perceived by some customers as a non-strategic, commodity business. Emerson wasn't getting credit in the marketplace as a provider of comprehensive, engineered solutions. So they decided to do something about it.

PUTTING TOGETHER A BRAND BUILDING PROGRAM

In 1999, Kathy Button Bell was brought on-board as the company's first Chief Marketing Officer. She was allowed to recruit some heavy-duty partners to join her team: Interbrand for corporate identity work, DDB Chicago for advertising and promotion, and Fleishman-Hillard for public relations. All of these are Omnicom Group companies.

The first order of business was market research. Working with Fleishman-Hillard and Interbrand, a multi-faceted study was designed to find out what various audiences felt about Emerson and its many business units. Using a combination of in-person and telephone interviews plus on-line employee surveys, the research produced three major findings:

- The need to better define Emerson and better describe the brand relationship between Emerson and its individual companies.
- The need to make Emerson's market leadership and technology prowess more visible.
- The need to make it easier for customers to understand the company and therefore make it easier to do business with Emerson.

The research clearly drove creation of Emerson's first brand promise:

"Emerson is where technology and engineering come together to create solutions for the benefit of our customers, driven without compromise for a world in action."

The next step was devising a new brand architecture system to better organize Emerson's vast portfolio of businesses. Interbrand recommended an "overbrand" approach, grouping all sixty-plus divisions into eight business (brand) platforms. In each case, "Emerson" was the common major descriptor. (See examples in the Brand Architecture chapter, page 17.)

This meant divisions that previously went to market using names like Fisher Valves, Rosemount transmitters and Micro Motion meters were now part of Emerson Process Management. They still promote the Fisher, Rosemount and Micro Motion brands, but Emerson is the overbrand.

Similarly, Copeland compressors, White-Rodgers thermostats and Alco solenoid valves became part of Emerson Climate Technologies. This process was repeated in each of the eight business platforms.

CREATING THE NEW LOOK

The third step involved creating a new logo with a distinctive double helix symbol. The old one was a big, industrial "E" complete with lightning bolt. It was only thirty years old, but it looked and felt older.

They also decided to drop the word "Electric" from the logo, because the company was so much more than that now.

Interestingly, business school grad students played a part in selecting the new logo. Through on-line research, they were shown six logo possibilities (including the incumbent logo) and asked to describe what each logo connoted. The winning logo was the one that best conveyed the key attributes that Button Bell and her team wished to associate with the Emerson brand.

The fourth step was to create a tagline that would help Emerson leverage its technology leadership and begin the transformation to being perceived as a more customer-driven company. The simple, but straightforward slogan DDB came up with was "Emerson. Consider It Solved."

EMERSON. CONSIDER IT SOLVED.™

This slogan helped reposition Emerson from a manufacturer of components to a provider of integrated solutions. Used with permission.

THE INTERNAL LAUNCH

The fifth step—the one many companies skip—was to launch the branding program to Emerson employees. The first half of 2001 was devoted to this. Employee meetings, branding seminars, intranet websites, plus elegant "We Are Emerson" brochures and powerful videos all helped Emerson employees understand the new direction.

"Sure, we had some resistance, but most people understood the objectives and jumped quickly onboard," said Button Bell. "In fact, once the shock of the new brand platform approach was absorbed, many managers said it was long overdue."

Part of the internal effort was a "Consider It Solved" Award program to formally recognize an individual or team who best exemplified the new philosophy. This award might be presented for going the extra mile to improve a product or service, creating a cross-divisional customer solution or solving a difficult customer problem.

THE EXTERNAL LAUNCH

The sixth step was to begin the external launch. It started slowly with airport dioramas in September of 2001, followed by a modest trade and business media campaign in the second quarter of 2002. Publications like *Wall Street Journal, Business Week* and *Forbes* were used. Total first year media spending was less than $3 million.

Public relations activities were ramped up, too. For the first time ever, an Emerson CEO (Dave Farr) appeared on national television talking about Emerson business strategies. His New York media tour included stops at CNBC (Squawk Box), Bloomberg and Reuters.

They also created a format so that divisional business groups could convert existing ads by simply changing the bottom portion to feature the new tagline and logo. This was the first time I was aware (early 2002) that something big was happening at Emerson. As part of an annual competitive ad review for one of my Houston-based valve clients, we mounted all competitive ads on black poster boards and lined a conference room wall with them. The Emerson ads immediately stood out due to the bold "Consider It Solved" color bar along the bottom.

This is one of several magazine ads produced in 2003 for Emerson's 2004 corporate branding program. © Emerson. Used with permission.

The seventh step was to aggressively expand the advertising effort in the Spring of 2003 to focus on FORTUNE 1000 company travelers with more airport "spectaculars" (large dioramas), business magazine print ads and drivetime business radio (CBS News with Charles Osgood).

THE EARLY RETURNS ARE IMPRESSIVE

So what does Emerson have to show for all this effort? It's still early, but the returns are already starting to roll in. For the first time, Emerson cracked the *FORTUNE* 50 list of world's most admired companies in 2003.

Readers of *CONTROL* magazine have moved Emerson to the top spot in technology leadership, up from number four in 1997. *INFORMATION WEEK* readers have boosted Emerson to #2 among e-business systems suppliers, up from #26 last year and #50 the year before.

But the most gratifying measure of success is that customers are starting to describe Emerson as a "solutions" company, and divisions are actively working together to solve customer problems with recommendations that cut across departmental lines.

According to a recent benchmark study by Wirthlin Worldwide, customers increasingly see Emerson as a "singular leader" (only a few points behind Sony and GE). And in market segments that have been emphasized in the company's early promotional efforts, Emerson actually comes out on top.

Internal studies show that 94% of Emerson employees believe the new brand platform is important to their long-term success, and 87% believe it helps them deliver more value to customers. Half of all Emerson employees feel the company is now more customer-focused than it was two years ago.

Another change is in the area of "marquee" accounts. Cross-divisional sales teams, working within the new brand platforms, have increased sales to large, corporate accounts by 700% versus the prior year (2003 versus 2002).

"The new business generated by these marquee account teams alone could make the branding and communications work pay for itself," said Button Bell. "Certainly, the silo mentality is lessening. We're replacing it with a passionate resolve to do what's right for the customer. Anything less is not acceptable."

And so, going back to our opening riddle—What do you get when you combine all those things? If you do it right, you get one enormous problem-solving machine, that's what. One that adds value for customers and shareholders alike.

IMAGINATION AT WORK: THE GENERAL ELECTRIC STORY

As I mentioned in the Introduction section of this book, General Electric was my branding epiphany back in 1999. I was innocently sitting in a hotel conference room full of business-to-business marketing and advertising people, minding my own business, when suddenly a freight train named Richard Costello came along and blasted me into the ditch.

As I recall, his exact words were "General Electric generates *incremental* revenue of ten billion dollars every year due to the power of our brand." Several years later, when I tracked the since-retired Costello down to explain those words, he tried his best to wiggle out of them. But there was no uncertainty in his voice that morning he first uttered them in San Jose.

A TEN BILLION DOLLAR BONUS

His primary point, even though he didn't put it in these exact words, was that GE received a bonus of $10 billion dollars in 1999, which was roughly equal to the company's entire net income that year. And if you consider their '99 sales revenues of $111.6 billion, we're saying that almost 10% of sales was a gift from something called brand power.

As those words started to sink in, my mind exploded with possibilities for companies I worked with back in Texas. How could they put brand power to work for them? How could I convince them it wasn't about having better features and benefits? How could I show them the error of starting and stopping ad programs on a whim? You know, wishful thinking stuff.

Later that year, I stumbled across Fort Worth–based Acme Brick, another example of a business-to-business marketer that was receiving roughly a 10% bonus due to the power of its brand. And Acme was a reasonably small company with annual sales of only $200 million (see case study, page 79) so I was starting to see that branding could work for companies of all sizes.

141

BRAND POWER AT WORK

In his 1999 talk, Costello used GE engineered plastics and jet engines as examples of product groups where the company was able to exert considerable marketing leverage due to its reputation, broad product line and trusted technology. GE's Lexan® performance polymers have enjoyed price premiums for many years, and Lexan brand power has allowed GE to form exclusive working relationships with leading plastics molders, automotive manufacturers and consumer electronics companies. When Apple introduced its shockingly bright "iMac" computers in red, orange, aqua and other unexpected hues, GE gave them a one-year exclusive on the Lexan color palette. So much for putty beige.

But as I said in the Introduction, the example I remember best from Costello's presentation was the simplest one—for GE Soft White light bulbs. Light bulbs are not exactly high technology—they've been around since 1879. And I can't imagine any shopper stopping to consider whether or not the manufacturer of any particular brand of light bulbs has got the essential process down pat. At least on the surface, it would seem, a light bulb is a light bulb is a light bulb.

And yet, when you walk in a grocery store to the light bulb section, there you'll find GE Soft White bulbs proudly displayed next to competitive light bulbs and the generic store brand. The performance specifications are identical. The store brand is usually about a third less, but amazingly, most people reach for the GE brand.

Why is that? Are we deliberately wasting money? Or is it because we think the GE product represents the better buy? Maybe we think the GE bulbs will last longer or burn brighter. Maybe we trust the GE brand more.

IT'S ALL ABOUT TRUST

That's what Costello thinks it is. He says the GE brand is all about trust. That's why consumers are willing to pay just a bit more for GE quality and dependability. And that's why it doesn't strike us as odd that the same brand is found on simple, everyday things like refrigerators and light fixtures, as well as on services like dental plans and financing agreements, and even on sophisticated business-to-business products like medical imaging systems and gas turbines.

When we see the General Electric monogram, we immediately assume the product or service is worthy of our trust. That's our expectation, pure and simple.

In the jet engines business, for example, all three of the major competitors (Rolls Royce, Pratt & Whitney and GE) have strong brands and similar technology claims. Costello says very little profit is made on engine sales. The big prize is the service contract after the equipment purchase, and that's where the GE trust factor becomes extremely important.

"In jet engines, our brand is often the tie-breaker," said Costello. "It says that we stand behind our product better, and that GE is not only the safe choice, but the best value decision."

THE NORMAN ROCKWELL COMPANY

Costello reports that GE began tracking this "trust factor" as far back as the 60s. In 1985, new techniques were adopted to compare GE scores with other large companies, like Microsoft, IBM, AT&T, Ford and General Motors.

In Costello's eyes, GE's image was like a Norman Rockwell painting—old fashioned, family-oriented, we'll always be there for you. The long-time slogan, "We Bring Good Things To Life," was a perfect fit for General Electric in the 80s and 90s. It also helped CEO Jack Welch's growth-by-acquisition strategy, because many takeover candidates were actually eager to become part of that kind of organization.

We bring good things to life.

For more than 20 years, this well-known theme symbolized trust for General Electric products and services. In 2002, the company gave it up for a new slogan emphasizing innovation. Used with permission.

But things change. Costello retired. Welch retired. General Electric stopped growing in double digit chunks. The stock price dropped 50%. And new CEO Jeff Immelt decided a different agenda was in order.

The missing link, according to Immelt was innovation. General Electric had stopped emphasizing growth from internally developed new technology. And even in areas where GE led the industry in technical breakthroughs, the company really wasn't getting full credit for that innovation. I guess it doesn't compute that the Norman Rockwell company can launch paradigm-shifting ideas into the great unknown.

THE SHIFT TO HIGHER TECHNOLOGY

So Immelt got his marketing and research people together and laid down the challenge: generate 7% incremental growth from new, internally developed technologies within three years. That translates to $9 billion in new money from innovation.

To accelerate the process, he appointed Beth Comstock as chief marketing officer. Comstock and Immelt told GE's eleven business unit marketing managers they had 60 days each to come back with five new ideas for growth businesses that would generate at least $100 million in sales within three years. He told them to think big and swing for the fences.

Of the 50+ ideas submitted by the eleven GE divisions, 35 were given the green light. Everything from wind-powered energy systems to sophisticated airport security systems using medical scanning technology to lightweight airplane engines that will power the air taxi market of tomorrow. (If there is an air taxi market.)

From a technology development standpoint, the wheels of change were put in motion in late 2003. Comstock actually started addressing the image problems earlier than that. Working with BBDO, GE's agency of 80 years (how's that for an amazing relationship?), Comstock made the very unpopular decision that "We Bring Good Things To Life" had to go in the latter part of 2002.

IMAGINATION AT WORK

Talk about risk! The second-guessers were going to have a field day. All that goodwill, all that brand equity down the drain. Comstock and BBDO were proposing that GE start calendar 2003 fresh with a totally new slogan: "Imagination At Work."

To support new CEO Jeff Immelt's emphasis on internally developed innovation, this theme was introduced in early 2003. Used with permission.

"Lighting and appliances account for less than 6% of GE sales," says Judy Hu, Global Executive Director for Advertising and Branding, "yet these are the products with which most people associate the company." Not exactly a solid foundation for innovation.

Hu said the decision was made to launch the re-branding effort with products and services that better reflected the company's new emphasis on technology development.

A decision was also made to use humor to soften GE's image and make the company appear more contemporary. Humorous approaches helped bridge the gap from the previous generation of ads, because several of the initial *Imagination At Work* TV spots used spoofs of traditional trust-related icons to deliver the new innovation messages.

For example, family-favorite Lassie was given computer-generated karate skills to protect Timmy from mountain lions and bears in an ad for GE Security Technologies. In another spot for GE Healthcare, a surgeon gets temporarily lost in an imaginary brain voyage a la Star Trek. He snaps out of it when an assistant says, "You said we've got to get back to the ship."

In addition to the expected broadcast media (GE owns 80% of the recently merged NBC Universal, after all), GE print ads also ran in general business publications like *The Wall Street Journal, The New York Times, Business Week, Forbes* and *Fortune*, as well as trade magazines like *Power Engineering, Building Operation Management, Plastics Technology and Automotive Design & Production*.

IMAGINATION ON THE WEB

Another early success in the Imagination At Work campaign was a website gimmick called "Viral Pen," which was developed by interactive shop AtmosphereBBDO. This allowed website visitors to access a pen, choose a color and draw a picture, which they could then e-mail to a friend. Forty-three million people tried the program in its first six months.

Now a new generation program allows you to invite several friends to draw along with you in real time. "Our challenge was to bring 'Imagination At Work' online," said Andreas Combuechen, CEO and Chief Creative Officer for AtmosphereBBDO. "The viral component empowered users to put their own imagination to work, and it also enabled us to demonstrate GE's 'wow' technology."

In fact, everything in GE's highly integrated communications effort has emphasized the "Wow" factor of GE technology. Creatively, the print ads are unimpressive. Collectively, however, the emphasis on technology is compelling.

Forty-three million people tried GE's "Viral Pen" website promotion during its first six months. Used with permission.

THE EARLY RESULTS

So what does GE have to show for this ambitious endeavor? It's very early, and they are reluctant to provide specifics, but it's obvious they are on the right track.

According to Hu, perception of GE as an innovative company has increased 35% in the first year. GE's scores as a "provider of high-tech solutions" is up 40%. And customer perceptions of GE as a "dynamic" company are up 50%.

And financial performance is up, too. The most recent quarter saw eight of eleven GE divisions experience double digit earnings growth again. Revenues are up 15% over the prior year, and the stock price is starting to move in the right direction.

It takes a lot of guts to get rid of a classic slogan like "We bring good things to life." It's not easy following in the footsteps of a business legend like Jack Welch. But Jeff Immelt, Beth Comstock and their colleagues at GE are making the tough decisions and reshaping their brand image for the good of the company's future. I guess that's why they make the big bucks, huh?

FROM PRODUCT LEADER TO INDUSTRY LEADER: THE HOBART STORY

Most marketing people would be quite happy working for a well-established 100+ year old company with a reputation for outstanding product quality. Most would be satisfied with increasing sales figures and consistent profits.

And wouldn't it be thrilling to have commanding market shares in virtually every category in which you compete? Most marketing managers might think so. But not the marketing people at Hobart Corporation.

Even though Hobart was the across-the-board leader in food service, cooking and cleaning equipment for commercial and institutional markets, it still had formidable competitors in each individual category. And on any given day, with this fragmented playing field, it seemed like some one was gaining ground. At least the opportunity was there.

LEVERAGING THE WINGSPAN

The management group at Hobart wanted to leverage the "broad wingspan" of its product leadership into a position only they could occupy. "We wanted to elevate the company from product leader to industry leader, and harness the intellectual capital that comes with being a business partner with our customers," said Dean Landeche, former Vice President of Brand Marketing for Hobart.

No other company had as much product and application knowledge. Nobody else had the broad perspective. And certainly no one was in a better position to determine and disseminate "best practices" for the food industry.

It was an opportunity they could not afford to pass up.

As 1997 approached, the first order of business was for Hobart to find a capable marketing and advertising services partner. After a formal search, the company selected HSR Business To Business Inc. (formerly Hensley Segal Rentschler) located in Cincinnati.

THINGS THAT KEEP CUSTOMERS AWAKE

A key part of the agency's winning presentation was for Hobart to develop a list of important things that their customers worry about. After a series of management retreats with the agency, this evolved into "Six Things That Keep Customers Awake At Night." The list covered everything from broad topics like food safety, energy consumption and labor costs to specific things like shrinkage and application of new technology. The sixth area involved ways for customers to grow sales.

As the list grew with additional detail and suggestions, ways to exploit the list quickly focused. And most of these strategies fell under the

The paradigm shift at Hobart was to quit talking about product innovations and start talking about things that customers were struggling with. Used with permission.

general heading of public relations, which was also a crucial plank in HSR's recommended approach.

"Not only was the marketplace fragmented," says HSR CEO Rick Segal, "but Hobart's marketing efforts were divided among three business groups and more than 30 product categories. Everybody was doing his or her own thing. We wanted to create a more unified voice for Hobart, and we saw dozens of opportunities to start making this happen."

It was determined that the voice of Hobart was to speak:

- With a strong point of view
- As an inspirational, authoritative leader
- As a unifying force and a source of best practices concerning major issues in the food service industry
- With a platform of credibility built upon delivering a broad base of solid, industry-leading equipment for 100+ years.

BUILDING THE BRAND WITH PUBLIC RELATIONS

"We wanted to make public relations activities the core of our branding program for Hobart," said HSR EVP Michael Hensley, "with a strong emphasis on key food service industry issues." They also wanted to identify Hobart in every possible way as a source of industry best practices.

This included the usual tactics like placing Hobart managers on industry conference agendas and writing feature articles for trade magazines. But the paradigm shift was to quit talking about product innovations and start talking about things that customers were struggling with.

The P.R. program also included a variety of unconventional strategies, like forming alliances with leading food industry consultants to swap content for websites (e.g., Hobart provides information on the total cost of equipment ownership, the consultant provides information on labor cost trends or food service operation productivity).

Hobart worked with major grocery chains to develop information on personnel training programs and equipment safety. And they sought out famous chefs like Emeril Lagasse and Wolfgang Puck to write menu suggestions and food preparation tips.

The result was a lively Hobart website, teeming with interesting content and linked to virtually everything a customer might need in the food industry.

In 1997, Hobart and HSR launched a proprietary magazine called SAGE (seasoned advice for food industry professionals). It started as a printed piece, and in 2001 evolved into an online, electronic publication.

SAGE magazine started as a printed piece and more recently has evolved to an online electronic publication to help identify Hobart as a company that tackles critical issues facing the food service industry. Used with permission.

Instead of being a threat to trade magazines, SAGE has been an ongoing source of usable news items for them. In fact, the July 2002 edition was co-produced with *Supermarket News* in both printed and electronic versions as part of that magazine's 75th anniversary.

FINDING GOOD CUSTOMER STORIES

For most B2B companies, getting ideas for feature articles out of the sales force is like pulling teeth, and it wasn't easy in the early going for Hobart. But as salespeople started to see the benefits of having their customers spotlighted in magazines and tradeshow program keynotes, the story suggestions gradually started to flow in.

A contest soliciting customer success stories generated more than 1,000 submissions, more than 200 of which were posted on the Hobart website. Used with permission.

One recent promotion, however, exceeded even the company's most optimistic expectations. Called "Here, There & Everywhere," the program's objective was to gather customer testimonials about Hobart equipment. The grand prize, which was to be awarded by random drawing, was a trip for two anywhere in the world. Monthly drawings were held throughout the contest for free sets of luggage.

More than 1,000 success stories were submitted. Two hundred and five entries in twelve market categories were eventually posted on the Hobart website (*www.hobartcorp.com*). Many of these expressed the attitude that customers love Hobart equipment like members of their family. It just doesn't get much better than that.

THE INDUSTRY LEADER DIFFERENCE

So what is the difference between product leader and industry leader? "One difference is we feel a whole lot closer to our customers now," said Landeche. "Not only have we worked with them on problems they feel are important, but in some cases, we know enough about how they are solving these problems to nominate them for key industry awards."

Landesche reported that Hobart has significantly increased its market share with large restaurant and hotel chains as these customers have consolidated and reduced the number of suppliers they use. Single product companies or ones with limited product lines are now at a decided disadvantage.

Hobart is carefully watching how it is perceived by customers, dealers and consultants. The first tracking study in 2001 showed increases in all but one of 35 factors, including significant jumps of 8-10 points in many areas. The number of respondents who felt Hobart was a source of unbiased industry trend and issue information was up 13 points. The number who said Hobart takes high profile positions on key issues facing the industry rose 23 points. And the number who felt Hobart was a source of "hot trend" information was up 13 points.

Foodservice Equipment & Supplies Magazine has awarded Hobart its "overall best in class" honor for three consecutive years, in addition to being selected best in numerous individual product categories. In receiving this award, Hobart was specifically recognized by food equipment dealers for "providing industry-leading support services and knowledgeable customer service."

It's interesting to note that Hobart is now spending *less* on advertising and marketing communications. Trade media spending was about half of its budget in 1997. Now it's about 30%. Roughly a third is spent on e-marketing projects, including the website and SAGE. Hobart budgets about 20% for public relations. Overall, annual marcom spending is less than $3 million, down about 10–15% over the past ten years.

BRAND PERSONALITY SHIFTS

Before the branding program began, Hobart's image might have been characterized as an "old, stodgy, conservative maker of high quality products." They were a sleeping giant that no one wanted to arouse.

Now the brand is associated with more desirable attributes, such as "passionate, concerned, thoughtful, responsive and accessible." By taking positions on critical industry issues, Hobart is now perceived to be more customer-focused. And more qualified to provide total equipment packages that include financing, training and installation assistance.

The company is even credited with having a sense of humor, thanks to the many award-winning ads and collateral pieces produced by HSR. One of my favorites is a darkly lit shot of an undercounter refrigerator in an alley with the headline, "If it were any tougher, it would beat you up and steal your lunch money."

All Hobart ads and brochures carry the tagline, "Solid equipment. Sound advice." which aptly sums up their problem-solving commitment to go well beyond the product-provider position.

POSTSCRIPT

In 2002, after several years of successful brand building, Hobart management took its eye off the ball. Faced with a severe economic downturn and internal pressure to meet sales objectives, the company shifted its emphasis from building the industry leader image to "one-off" sales promotions designed to stimulate short-term sales.

For example, a series of product ads featured 0% financing from American Express for qualified buyers. (See example ad in the Consistent Execution chapter, page 60.) They could have wrapped these special offers in an overall message of doing what the industry leader does to help its customers during hard times, but they didn't. They just dropped the industry leader messages and substituted promotional messages.

So they shouldn't have been too surprised when a 2004 tracking study showed their leadership scores down in every category. Having learned this painful lesson, Hobart has rededicated itself to supporting the brand in every marketing communications effort. A new policy is now in place requiring all communications programs to be coordinated by Brand Marketing.

Portions of this case study are reprinted with permission from *Marketing News*, October 14, 2002.

SELLING SOLUTIONS INSTEAD OF MACHINES: THE IBM STORY

In 1993, the computer industry was splintering into thousands of horizontally oriented companies serving only a narrow slice of a customer's total needs (storage devices, database software, personal computers, servers, mainframes, etc.). Newly appointed IBM CEO Lou Gerstner made a key observation based on his previous experience as a *customer* of information technology: somebody has to connect all this stuff and make it work!

He felt that IBM's size and combination of hardware, software and technology know-how would uniquely position the company to take advantage of that customer need. So despite the prevailing assumption that IBM would save itself from financial ruin by selling off pieces of the company, he decided not to.

It was a gutsy decision, because IBM was in the process of losing $800 million in the first four months of 1993 alone. IBM stock had dropped from a high of $43 a share in 1987 to $13 a share by the time Gerstner took office on April 1st of that year.

THE END APPEARS TO BE NEAR

Everywhere Gerstner went, the message was the same: "rapidly declining mainframe sales, prices that were much higher than those of IBM competitors, a lack of participation in the rapidly growing client/server segment and an alarming decline in the company's image."

Editors and industry experts were proclaiming IBM's days as an industry leader to be over. The company was washed up, an also-ran, an embarrassment to America and the world of computer technology. And it was hemorrhaging cash—in danger of running out of money altogether.

Many people assumed the Little Tramp was headed for the boxcar to hitch a ride out of town.

But not Lou Gerstner. He challenged all of his top managers to start spending more time face-to-face with customers, asking them what it would take to solve their problems and win more business. His team

In the early 1990s, IBM was identified with selling computer hardware like this System 390 set-up. Used with permission.

immediately tackled the daunting task of shaking up and right–sizing the bureaucracy, and restoring profitability to IBM.

SPEAKING WITH ONE VOICE

In June 1993, Gerstner hired Abby Kohnstamm as head of corporate marketing for IBM. She had worked for him previously at American Express. Kohnstamm spent several months doing a situation analysis and found that, while the IBM brand was strong, the hodge podge of messages and creative approaches coming from more than 70 different agencies was unacceptable. It also contributed to the reign of fiefdoms, with each operating unit having its own agency and its own ad budget.

So in June 1994, IBM shocked the advertising world by consolidating its advertising account at a single agency, Ogilvy & Mather, that had never worked for IBM. Maybe shock is too soft a word.

But Kohnstamm, like Gerstner and the other top executives, saw the opportunity to position IBM as a provider of "seamless, easy solutions that tie products together and solve problems." And she knew it would take integrated communications with a capital "I" in order to accomplish that tall objective.

MAKING BIG BLUE APPROACHABLE

Later that year, O&M debuted its "Subtitles" campaign that featured a series of humorous vignettes about elderly Frenchmen, Czech nuns and Greek fishermen solving problems with the help of IBM. The tagline was "Solutions for a Small Planet."

According to O&M CEO Shelly Lazarus, the element of surprise was intentional. "When you're trying to change people's perceptions, you must violate what they think they know about the brand," he said.

For the first time, IBM advertising was developing the brand personality of a likable, helpful, very smart company that gets things done—even for small customers. And IBM products were conspicuously absent in the advertising. The emphasis was on solutions, not specific products.

AN ARMY OF CONSULTANTS

By 1996, services had been split out from sales as a separate business called IBM Global Services. IBM service consultants were undergoing special training to re-think their "brand promise" and re-program themselves to sell solutions instead of machines.

In his book, *Brand Asset Management*, Scott Davis tells of training over 3,000 IBM employees to act like value-adding consultants. In order to gain credibility early on, they had to include at least two non-IBM recommendations in every proposal. It drove the IBM sales group crazy.

Ultimately, however, it worked because customers started getting comfortable with the idea that IBM consultants weren't just out to sell more IBM hardware. IBM service revenues grew from $7.8 billion in 1992 to $19.3 billion in 1997.

EXPLORING THE NEW FRONTIER

By that time, the Internet was starting to capture people's imaginations, and IBM was determined to jump on that horse and ride for all it was worth.

"It was like the wild west," said Maureen McGuire, V.P. Integrated Marketing Communications for IBM. "People were thinking they had to be on the Internet, but they weren't sure why."

In October 1997, the "e-Business" campaign was created to target technology influencers in small and large businesses. IBM didn't coin the

In 1997, IBM took another step to position itself as the undisputed leader in integrated computer systems solutions with the "e-Business" campaign. Used with permission.

term, but it did take it from relative obscurity to front and center in every businessperson's mind.

In launching this initiative, Kohnstamm had three objectives:

- Become the thought leader in Internet-related applications
- Position IBM as the only end-to-end solutions provider
- Promote the fact that IBM has more e-business engagements than anyone

By 1998, services accounted for 29% of IBM's $82 billion in annual revenues, and even though total revenues in '98 were up only 4% versus the prior year, service revenues were up 22%. Services actually accounted for 39% of IBM's pre-tax profits, an amazing turnaround from the earliest years of Gerstner's tenure when services was a money-losing operation.

And equally of note, almost half of IBM's service revenues during this time were from long-term outsourcing deals where IBM assumed ownership and total responsibility for a client's IT operations. IBM had truly arrived as a legitimate competitor to traditional IT outsourcing kingpins like EDS and Andersen/Accenture, and in many significant cases, it was beating them at their own game.

THE MOST INCREDIBLE MAKEOVER EVER

As one industry observer wryly noted, "IBM is now IBS, where 'S' is for services, software and solutions." Machines were clearly taking a back seat.

And the white-shirted, stodgy old company was clearly taking on a new personality as a hip, wise-cracking computer wizard that could solve your information technology problems. And keep you from bumping into other problems you hadn't as yet encountered.

It was probably the most incredible personality makeover in the history of business. In five years, IBM went from washed up has-been on the brink of bankruptcy, to industry leader in the most desirable position of integrated services leader.

In 1993, IBM had almost 100% brand awareness, but next to zero brand equity because customer expectations about IBM were causing them to move in opposite directions. The IBM brand had little or no value, and the company's future prospects looked grim.

A decade later, the 2004 *Business Week*/Interbrand Global Brand Scorecard now ranks IBM number three with an estimated brand value of $53.8 billion.

To paraphrase Mark Twain, it would appear that the reports of its death were greatly exaggerated.

FROM ANONYMOUS TO OMNIPOTENT: THE INTEL STORY

Most business-to-business sales and marketing managers I've ever worked with are confident they know who their customers are. Before 9/11, if you had something really important to say to your customers, you would just buy a plane ticket and go see them. Now you arrange a teleconference.

That was pretty such the situation with Intel in the late 1980s. They had a dozen or so large OEM computer manufacturer customers, and they had become very good at meeting the technical performance needs of those customers. "Our design engineers would go meet with their design engineers to determine what was needed," said Dennis Carter, former V.P. Marketing for Intel, "and then we'd figure out how to make it work for them."

Within these dozen companies, Intel was hugely important. To everybody else, however, Intel was virtually anonymous. In 1982, Intel introduced the 16-bit 80286 microprocessor, which was very successful and widely adopted as the early workhorse chip for personal computers. In 1985, they introduced the 32-bit 386 chip, which was supposed to replace the 286. It was three times faster and offered sophisticated multitasking capabilities.

HELPING DEMAND KEEP UP WITH SUPPLY

However, it was also a lot more expensive than the 286, so market acceptance of the 386 DX was slower than anticipated. To combat this, Intel brought out a less expensive 386 SX chip in 1988. The problem, which you may be starting to detect, is that Intel was making technological advances faster than their OEM customers could create demand for them. The 386 SX was cheaper, but it didn't help expand the market for Intel; it simply cannibalized sales of the DX chip. The result was lost revenue opportunities for Intel.

In 1989, Intel started to broaden its communications horizons to include "retail" computer buyers as well as computer makers and MIS professionals.

Intel's first branding system was based on numbers which identified the microprocessor chip inside. The objective here was to prompt end-users to ask for the better performing chip. © Intel Corporation. Used with permission.

Most retail computer buyers had no idea what made personal computers work–they relied on the reputation of computer manufacturers like IBM, Compaq, Epson and others for that. So it was quite a shock when Intel started running magazine ads and billboards with a huge red "x" sprayed graffiti-style over the numbers "286" and encouraging consumers to consider the improved performance of "386 SX" powered computers.

Intel was killing its very successful 286 chip with an even better one, forcing its OEM accounts to get with the newer technology program. According to Chip Shafer, head of the small Irvine, CA-based agency that produced those revolutionary ads, the program was so successful Intel had to take a mothballed wafer lab in Livermore, CA out of retirement. But the real key, Shafer pointed out, was when every computer maker introduced new 386 SX powered models and included the 386 SX designation as part of *their* product names. Now, for the first time, PCs were starting to be referred to by the Intel chip inside.

WHEN A TRADEMARK IS NOT REALLY A TRADEMARK

And this might have been the end of the story, except that Intel was ready to launch an even better chip (the 486) at the same time that Intel competitors were announcing their own processors using the Intel numbering system. Since Intel had not licensed the 386 technology to anyone, and because the competitive chips were claiming 386 performance without being able to deliver on that promise, Intel naturally thought this was a violation of its pending trademarks.

Unfortunately, the courts decided otherwise. As Dennis Carter recalls the story, "It was a somber Friday afternoon in March of 1991 when we got the bad news on the lawsuit. Within several hours, CEO Andy Grove was in my office telling me we couldn't use the numerical product identification system anymore. He wanted to see my recommendations on a new "branding" strategy the following Monday."

THE COMPUTER INSIDE

Luckily, Carter had already been doing some experimentation with different creative approaches in various markets around the globe. Working with his domestic ad agency, Dahlin Smith White (now part of Euro RSCG), a campaign using the theme "Intel: The Computer Inside" was already in the early stages of creative development.

But Carter wanted something more succinct, so he adapted a line from Intel's Japanese agency, Dentsu, using the words "Intel In It" and combined this with the computer inside idea. That's how "Intel Inside" came to be. Carter even appropriated a swirl logo developed for the Japanese market, and the familiar "Intel Inside" logo was born.

Certainly, one of the objectives for "Intel Inside" was to make the processor #1 on an IT manager's wish list of things that go in a PC purchase. But it went far beyond that, because now consumers at large

This magazine ad helped launch the "Intel Inside" program to value-added resellers and personal computer users. © Intel Corporation. Used with permission.

This scene from the first Intel TV spot challenged computer users to think about internal components for the first time. © Intel Corporation. Used with permission.

were becoming aware of a processor's importance in making a PC do what it's supposed to do.

That's why the first TV spot, produced in the fall of 1991 to help launch the next generation 486 chip, was a computer-animated "flyover" that allowed viewers to see inside a personal computer. At the end of the flyover was a neon sign indicating "vacancy here" room for future expansion. Up to this point, we didn't even care what was inside a computer, and now all of a sudden we're worried about having room for future expansion!

As you might guess, Intel's traditional OEM customers were more than a little concerned about the power shift from their own brand dominance to a marketplace where consumers specified PCs by the microprocessor inside. Kevin Lane Keller, in his book *Strategic Brand Management*, tells the story well:

> *IBM was the first major OEM to use the Intel Inside logo. With the introduction of its first 486-based PC in April, 1991, IBM offered to use the new logo—still in draft form. Intel faxed IBM a rough drawing for its use in the ad. IBM would not tell Intel where on the ad it would be located, and all the Intel marketing task force could do was hope for prominent, high visible placement. In fact, the Intel Inside logo was clearly visible in the ad layout. After running this ad, however, IBM did not use the Intel Inside logo again for nearly a year.*

In any event, the race was on to jump on the Intel Inside bandwagon. Within six months, over 300 OEMs had signed co-op agreements to

use the Intel Inside promotional materials. More than 100 of these companies were featuring the Intel Inside logo in their ads, taking advantage
of 50-50 co-op matching funds up to a maximum of 3% of Intel
purchases.

BIG INVESTMENT, BIG RETURNS

By 1994, when computer makers were putting CD-ROM drives in most
PCs, Intel had expanded its annual budget to more than $200 million
to include broad-based and more expensive consumer media. Industry
estimates generally agreed that Intel invested approximately $500 million
in the Intel Inside program the first three years, and the budget rapidly
escalated to more than $700 million annually toward the end of the mil-
lennium.

So what do you get for that kind of money? Well, using 1991 as the
base year, Intel revenues increased six fold by 2000 (to $33.7 billion) and
earnings almost doubled that rate of increase (to $10.5 billion). *Business
Week's* most recent ranking of the world's most valuable brands shows
Intel at #5 with an estimated value of $33.5 billion.

But, in my opinion, the primary return on that sizeable investment is
that Intel has created a viable, dynamic brand personality that virtually
anyone who has anything to do with computers can define in a way
gives Intel a decided marketing advantage. If it has "Intel Inside" it must
be good. It must be state-of-the-art. It must be high-performing.

And if you're an Intel competitor, that must look like a pretty steep
hill to climb.

FROM SELLING TO MARKETING: THE JAMES HARDIE STORY

Sydney, Australia-based James Hardie Industries introduced its fiber cement siding products in the United States in 1989, using conventional sales techniques to demonstrate the product to leading builders, lumber yards and home improvement centers.

It was slow going, and even though the product was guaranteed for 50 years not to rot or crack, many builders hated it. It was heavy to install, ate saw blades for lunch, and it showed every flaw in a bad framing job.

Plus, there were other fiber cement products on the market, so the question ultimately came back to, "What's your best price?"

In 1997, after frustrating meetings with several of the big box home improvement centers, James Hardie USA president Lewis Gries had an epiphany. He realized the only way to differentiate his siding product and get the profit margin it deserved was through a brand-building program.

Together with John Dybsky (then an independent marketing consultant, now marketing director for brands at James Hardie) he launched a nationwide search for an agency to develop a branding program for a business-to-business product. The agency selected, Sawyer Riley Compton of Atlanta, GA, was challenged with laying the foundation for this effort with a test market budget of only $500,000.

THE TEST MARKET PROGRAM

"The first step was to do some research to find out what homeowners thought about the building materials used in their homes," said SRC CEO Louis Sawyer. "Our assumption was that siding was a low-interest category, but that turned out not to be correct."

What the research revealed was that people get emotional about their homes, and if you focus on what building materials can *provide* (safety, security, warmth, stability) rather than what they actually *are*, home buyers care a lot.

This insight was combined with consumer buying predictions from Faith Popcorn's Brain Trust indicating that baby boomers were moving in the direction of "neotraditional" homes that mixed the best of modern construction with the look and feel of historic structures. The agency was now ready to start putting together an advertising strategy.

EMPHASIZING THE LIFESTYLE BENEFITS

Instead of concentrating the media budget in traditional homebuilder trade publications, SRC chose several lifestyle magazines, including *Southern Living*, *Sunset* and *Coastal Living*.

Product features take a backseat to lifestyle considerations in this ad promoting James Hardie siding products. © James Hardie Inc. Used with permission.

From a creative standpoint, ads emphasized the emotional appeal of houses made with strong, weather-resistant materials. The siding was visible, but it wasn't the first thing you noticed. For example, one ad featured a couple's bare feet propped up on a front porch railing with a pitcher of lemonade nearby. The headline was, "You put your life into a home. Then, moment by moment, it gives it all back."

Another ad pictured a young girl pulling her sister in a wagon in front of a house surrounded by a picket fence. The headline was, "Perhaps it's time to build the home you see every time you close your eyes."

Trade ads explained the brand position and merchandised the interest that was being generated on behalf of builders and remodeling contractors. Again, the siding was visible but it was always

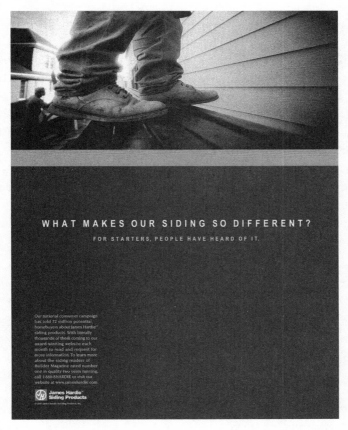

Trade ads for James Hardie siding products helped builders and remodeling contractors understand how the company was supporting their selling efforts. © James Hardie Inc. Used with permission.

shown with a builder's hands or feet in the foreground. One typical headline was, "Generic siding is fine. If you happen to be a generic builder."

Another trade ad showed a close up of a builder's well-worn work shoes next to a wall of siding. The headline was, "What makes our siding so different? For starters, people have heard of it." Copy referenced the brand's rapidly increasing awareness and preference among home buyers.

GETTING THE SALES FORCE ON BOARD

Another obstacle that had to be overcome was the James Hardie sales force. "They were good at calling on purchasing agents and talking price and delivery," Sawyer said, "but we knew this was a different kind of sell. We had to reach the marketing directors of major home builders and help them appreciate the value this effort could add to their sales program."

This required SRC to work closely with James Hardie sales managers to produce selling and promotional materials that explained the brand story. They also aggressively pursued co-branding opportunities, such as putting James Hardie siding on model homes and displays in builder design centers. Similarly, SRC sought Hardie product placements in "dream home" promotions sponsored by the various lifestyle magazines.

Hardie also emphasized co-op advertising programs with leading builders where the builder's ad message was blended skillfully along side a lifestyle photo of children and families frolicking in front of a James Hardie enclosed home. The tagline beneath the Hardie logo was "Why settle for vinyl?"

HELPING CUSTOMERS TELL THE DIFFERENCE

"When we started this program," Sawyer said, "the primary competitive product was vinyl siding, which was growing rapidly because it was supposed to last longer than wood." Builders liked it too, because it was lightweight and easy to install. But it just didn't look or feel like wood. It was thin and rattled when you thumped it, so Hardie built side-by-side displays and encouraged home buyers to do the "tap" test.

One-on-one research with home buyers pointed out repeatedly the problem they had with the "cheapness" of vinyl siding. When builders persisted in acting like homeowners wouldn't know the difference, this research turned them around quickly.

"Vinyl siding met the home buyer's functional requirements, but not the emotional ones," Sawyer said. "Our ads and displays spoke directly to the affluent baby boomer audience, and they appreciated the difference immediately."

MAKING THE CASH REGISTER RING

The result of all this effort is what we now know as "Hardiplank," the number one brand of siding in North America. Since 2000, James Hardie has nearly doubled its production capacity to keep up with demand, and acquired two of its competitors. Starting with one plant in 1990, the company now has eight plants with more than 1.8 billion square feet of manufacturing space.

North American sales for James Hardie Siding Products have increased from $122.8 million in 1997 (the year the brand building market test was started) to $476.9 million in 2003, a gain of 388%. Which means they have enjoyed a whopping 64% increase per year on average.

Brand awareness among builders has gone from less than 30% to more than 60% in four years. Awareness for all other siding products has stayed the same or decreased slightly. And James Hardie is now the third most-recognized brand of building material, which is incredible when you consider how many formidable competitors duke it out in that marketplace.

So the choice is clear: You can sell product features and low price to the trade, or you can blaze a path that makes it easy for end-users to understand, even demand the extra quality your product affords. And trade influences are more than happy to go along for the ride.

One is called selling, and the other is called marketing. And for some strange reason, the people who resist your selling overtures will welcome your marketing support with open arms. It's the miracle of branding.

Portions of this case study are reprinted with permission from *Marketing News*, May 27, 2002.

CASE STUDY 16

INVESTING IN DANCE LESSONS:
THE MEADWESTVACO TANGO
PAPER STORY

For some reason, most B2B marketers think marcom expenditures and results are a deep, dark secret to be stored securely in the company vault, like the formula for Coca Cola or Krispy Kreme doughnuts. As a result, business-to-business marketing communications has become a craft that is stuck in the Dark Ages, little understood, appreciated or trusted by top managers. In some cases it's a necessary evil, in others a discretionary indulgence. But in every case, it's an expense of the black hole variety.

Now, thanks to Gordon Hochhalter and Bob Goranson at Mobium Creative Group, Chicago, and their client, Marc Tannenbaum, marketing vp at MeadWestvaco, Stamford, CT., I'm pleased to provide another piece of evidence that marketing communications is, in fact, an investment. One that will pay significant dividends for the knowledgeable investor.

Our story begins in 1998 with an anonymous printing paper called TexCover II. The name was derived from "Texas" where it was made, and "Cover" which represented the majority of its applications (postcards, pocket folders, etc.). TexCover II had many redeeming qualities, most notably that it was easy for printers to use and very "forgiving" of on-press variation. Unfortunately, not enough people were aware of those qualities. TexCover II was stuck in fifth place in its category, with annual sales of less than $40 million.

TEACHING A WALLFLOWER TO DANCE

Enter the creative folks at Mobium, who conducted some basic customer research to find out what people thought of TexCover II (if they thought of it at all). Those who were regular users liked its consistent, predictable performance for the most part.

So the creative recommendation was to give the product a snappy name, Tango, and a memorable slogan, "Always performing," that put the spotlight on its favorable qualities. One of the introductory ads showed a coffee-drinking contortionist with the headline, "If you're looking for a

Two-sided inserts in printing and graphic arts trade magazines were used to demonstrate the "always performing" qualities of Tango paper. Used with permission.

challenge . . . don't use this paper." The reasons: quick and easy folding, flawless stamping, trimming and die-cutting. The summary copy line was, "Tango, the most forgiving C1S cover you can use."

Another early ad, which ran in printing industry trade publications like *Graphic Arts Monthly* and *Printing Impressions*, featured a father and son fire-eating team with the line, "If you like a little excitement now and then . . . don't use this paper." Why? Because it's stable, reliable, without defects or long drying times. You get the picture. Sales went up 27% the first year.

The second year they ad they expanded the product line, adding single and two-side coated versions. The creative was consistently brilliant, with insert ads showing a child in a fire truck on one side (I wanted to be a fireman), and a circus daredevil diving through a flaming hoop on the back (But I was born to perform). Each ad in the series paid off the "Always performing" theme with reasons that printers could appreciate—flawless finishes, stellar stamping, reliably gorgeous ink holdout, etc.

There was even a special website, www.tangopaper.com for all the details. Sales went up 34%.

FULLY INTEGRATED MARCOM SUPPORT

Along the way, collateral material and swatch books were produced, and an integrated direct mail campaign was aimed at mid-size printers. The website was customized to allow customers to request pre-cut paper samples or direct contact from a salesperson.

"The various elements of the campaign needed to be employed in such a way that they served to move the prospect along the purchase path," said Goranson.

There was an 800 telephone number for customers to locate the name of their nearest distributor. And training sessions were organized for the sales force to help them better understand the product positioning and take that message to the marketplace. Sales went up another 18%.

In the most recent advertising phase, trade magazine inserts featured distinctive, humorous illustrations by Mark Frederickson with apprehensive performers being helped along by the always performing Tango brand paper. Leon the Chameleon Comic avoids off-color performances (no blue hue, no yellow cast). Marty the Mental Marvel can actually fold socks with his mind (reliable die-cuts, folding and scoring).

Visuals from the "always performing" ad series were repeated on the swatch book and promotional materials distributed to printers and graphic artists. Used with permission.

TAKE THESE RESULTS TO THE BANK

And despite an industry-wide recession these past several years, Tango sales continued to climb, although at a more modest rate. The result is that these marketers have taken a number five also-ran product, and in four years turned it into a strong number two contender that is now pushing for category dominance.

Awareness of the Tango brand among printers has gone from zero to 67%. They have doubled the business, going from $40 to $80 million in annual sales. And they managed to increase distribution among mid-size and large sheet-fed printers, an area in which the product did not previously have a foothold. They have maintained profit margins in the midst of a difficult economic climate, too.

But here's the message you can take to your banker, or more importantly, to your CFO: to get an incremental $126 million in sales, MeadWestvaco invested only $2.0 million in all marketing communications activities over the four year period. That's a SIX THOUSAND percent return on investment. The product is essentially the same. The competition hasn't changed. The only thing that's different is the way the product is promoted.

It's amazing so many b-to-b marketers continue to overlook the marketing communications trump card, but they do. They've bought into the old wives tale that advertising is an expense. And they earnestly believe the way to protect the bottom line is to clamp down when times get tough.

In short, they just don't get it. Maybe this story will help change that, but I suspect we'll need more evidence. If you've got some locked away in your company vault, send me an email at lamons@ads2biz.com. I'd love to share it with other practitioners.

Portions of this case study are reprinted with permission from *Marketing News*, June 9, 2003.

THE POWER OF BLUE: THE MILLER ELECTRIC STORY

In 1993 Miller Electric, the number two manufacturer of welding equipment at that time, did a customer survey that revealed, among other things, how passionate welders were about their welding equipment. The survey also showed that welders regarded Miller as a trusted friend that could be counted on to help them do better welding jobs.

Miller decided to build their advertising program around these two observations. And one of the most successful B2B branding programs was born.

The category leader in 1993 was Lincoln Electric, known for its broad line of bright red welding equipment and accessories. Miller's products were blue. So somebody came up with the slogan, "The Power Of Blue." Hey, this branding stuff is easy, right?

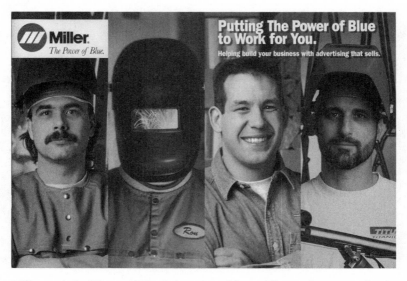

Miller made its "Power of Blue" slogan stand for welding equipment applications expertise and doubled the market share of its larger rival. Used with permission.

Well, not really. As we all know, slogans come and go. Some companies change slogans every time the sales manager has a wild hair. The difference in this case is the consistently powerful execution of the simple Miller slogan, and how the slogan has become stronger with each passing year.

GETTING CONTROL OF THE MEDIA SCHEDULE

But we're getting ahead of our story. In order to inject a little passion and trustworthiness into Miller advertising, some radical surgery had to be performed. At the time everyone in the welding industry was running lots of fractional page, 2-color ads in dozens and dozens of trade publications. Miller was spending $1.6 million each year in 127 publications.

One of the first acts by former marketing V.P. Tim DeMars was to cut the number of books to fourteen and the space budget to $550,000. You could hear howls of protest from the company's headquarters in Appleton, WI all the way to the Mexican border.

Miller started running full color pages and spreads exclusively. Gorgeous ads full of emotion and appealing graphics. Big, bold headlines with carefully chosen words to reach out and grab the target audience by the work shirt. Wimpy ads were shown the door.

For example, one spread ad had a bright red left hand page with a dainty "Roses are red" in fancy script. The right hand page was blue with a huge "Power sources are blue" in 120-pt. Helvetica Bold. Copy

Welders are passionate about their equipment and about doing good welding jobs. Miller ads were designed to play to that emotion. © Miller Electric. Used with permission.

encouraged welders to not just set the current, but set the standard with industry-leading power sources from Miller.

A totally different Miller ad from that period showed a young boy with his father and grandfather. The bold type headline was, "He's got his father's eyes. His grandfather's grit. And someday, he'll have their welders."

DRIVING CUSTOMERS TO THE WEBSITE

Not only did these ads grab attention, they generated results. Before the Power of Blue campaign started, Miller ads produced less than 1,000 sales leads per year. Immediately with the start of the new campaign, that number started to increase significantly and the volume has steadily risen every year since. Today, Miller generates more than 40,000 leads annually through all marcom activities.

Through these dramatic, skillfully crafted ads, Miller began to assume its position as an approachable, roll-up-the-sleeves partner you'd gladly invite along to the job site. As a logical extension of the partnering appeal, training programs became an essential part of the marketing mix. And as the Internet blossomed, on-line training programs were developed.

"The Internet has changed significantly the way people get information in the welding industry," observed DeMars. "Because of this, we were able to radically change our approach to many things, including tradeshows."

FROM TRADESHOWS TO TRADE FAIRS

Before the change, Miller spent more than $750,000 for tradeshow booth space and graphics. Now they spend about $65,000. The difference goes to sponsor regional "trade fairs" with distributors.

Miller has reduced the footprint of its tradeshow displays, often combining small divisional and distributor space with blue carpet that stretches across aisles to give the appearance that Miller has a lot more space than it really does. (The aisles are free.)

THE SOURCE OF WELDING KNOW-HOW

And public relations has become a key component of Miller marketing communications activities. One of the cornerstones of this is an in-house magazine called *Applied Welding*, which was first published in the 1940s. *Applied Welding*, which now has a circulation of 120,000 (more than double the leading welding trade magazine), is chock full of applications-oriented articles and features. Many of these stories are re-used for other public relations opportunities. (See example of Applied Welding in the chapter on Brand Positioning, page 36.)

"Because helping customers do a better welding job is key to Miller's image as a trusted partner, the Company puts a lot of effort into developing application stories and case histories," says Vickie Rhiner, Marketing Communications Manager for Miller. You won't find much brag and boast in *Applied Welding*. The emphasis is on how a particular piece of equipment saved a customer money or boosted his productivity.

Unlike many other companies that trot out new advertising themes every year like the latest model car, Miller has stayed consistently within the Power of Blue concept for more than a decade, and has no intention of changing. Miller has changed ad agencies, but not ad themes, and that says a lot.

PULLING AWAY FROM THE COMPETITION

"In the beginning, we had to deal with a lot of frustrated associates," said DeMars, "because we consolidated budgets and eliminated many pet

Welders can access hundreds of technical articles and success stories on the Miller website. Used with permission.

projects. But the opposition quickly went by the boards when we started to pull away from our competition."

The focused effort has produced many tangible rewards for Miller. In 1993, they were several market share points behind Lincoln Electric in the welding equipment field. By early 2004, Miller's share had more than doubled that of Lincoln.

And even though industry sales have been flat in recent years, Miller has more than doubled its sales, and profits have tripled over the past decade.

One more measurement—one that brings big smiles to the face of any Miller salesperson: in a recent study, more than 90% of welders surveyed were able to identify the color blue with Miller. Less than 50% were able to associate any other color with a competitor.

You can talk about the power of branding all you want, but in the welding equipment field, the "Power of Blue" is all you need to know.

SMALL COMPANY BRAND BUILDING: THE NEW PIG STORY

Usually when I think about companies that have achieved extraordinary results in building brand images for business-to-business products and services, I think of large companies such as General Electric, Caterpillar or IBM. In fact, people working for small enterprises often share the frustration that their meager resources are totally consumed by the basics of b-to-b marketing communications: brochures, trade shows, direct mail, and so on.

And I understand that frustration, at least to some extent. But just because you're up to your eyeballs in sales promotion requirements doesn't necessarily mean the kiss of death for branding. Here's a great example of a small company that started out 19 years ago with a brand-building attitude and has never wandered far from the path.

The company is called New Pig Corporation, and it's located in Tipton, PA (it would have been "The Pig Corporation" but surprisingly that name was taken when co-founder Ben Stapelfeld went to register with the secretary of state). New Pig's first and only product in 1985 was an absorbent sock, or "pig," which consisted of ground-up corn cob bits stuffed into panty hose to sop up machine oil spills on industrial plant floors.

PARTNERS IN GRIME

From the beginning, Stapelfeld and his partners decided to have fun with the company and its image. The toll-free 800 phone line was 1-800-HOT-HOGS. Customers were "partners in grime" (PIG). When the company developed enough products to produce a simple catalog, it was called a "Pigalog."

Occasionally, they went too far, like the time they produced a mailer with the headline "More suck for the buck." And Southerners didn't like Sparky, the company's pig character, dressed like Elvis either.

But most people liked the fun approach a lot. And because New Pig put the highest emphasis on responsiveness and listening, the product

Sparky is the spokespig for New Pig Corporation, helping create a friendly, responsive brand image for the company. Courtesy of New Pig Corporation. www.newpig.com. Used with permission.

line grew every time a customer asked for something special to solve another nasty leak or spill problem.

Today, the company offers more than 4,500 products, and it's the unquestioned leader in spill and leak containment—they created that category and they own it! The 2005 Pigalog is more than 400 pages and features more than 400 new products not included in the previous issue.

HOW ABOUT SOME DIRECT MARKETING?

But I'm getting ahead myself, because like most success stories, this one didn't happen overnight. Stapelfeld and his partners had bought the unprofitable industrial facility cleaning division of Downers Grove, Ill.-based ServiceMaster Co., thinking their "proprietary" absorbent sock would make a big difference. Most of the 64 franchisees thought it was a joke. Forty eight left immediately, and the rest were gone soon thereafter. First-year sales were only $350,000.

So New Pig decided to try direct marketing. They bought a list of 3,000 plant maintenance people and New Pig mailed them a special

"Box of Seven" absorbent socks mailer. The sample products were sent free of charge in September 1985 along with an offer to request an additional 40 socks for a 45-day free trial. One hundred people took them up on the special offer. After the trial period, each prospect was called to see if he or she was satisfied, and if so, sent an invoice for $78. The customer still had 30 days to pay, so it was actually 75 days net.

By December, the direct mail program had risen to 25,000 names and was simply a letter offering 40 socks for a 45-day no-obligation trial. Six months later, the mailing program had accelerated to 250,000 names, and the New Pig direct marketing program was off and running.

PUTTING ON A HAPPY SNOUT

The thing that makes the New Pig story different, however, is the distinctive personality the owners created for the company. It would have been much easier to play it safe and emphasize product features or low price. And I'm sure they did plenty of that, but they went further.

Their corporate personality made customers want to come back for more. They invented cartoon characters, such as "Squeal Armstrong" (first pig on the moon), "Hambo, "Pigmalion" and "Chief Sitting Boar." They gave away pig hats with snouts, ears and curly pigtails. And "Oink" T-shirts. And "pigskin" footballs. And, of course, piggy banks and cuddly stuffed pigs.

The latest brainstorm is "Sooo-e-mail" where you register to receive automatic e-mail notification for new products and special offers.

"Oinkle Sam" is one of dozens of pig-oriented characters created by New Pig to develop the brand personality. Courtesy of New Pig Corporation. Used with permission.

GETTING CUSTOMERS IN ON THE ACT

Magazine editors loved the freshness of the New Pig approach, and company representatives were soon being portrayed as industry spokespersons for an industry that New Pig was, in fact, creating as it went along.

Every Pigalog included customer testimonials, many with innovative suggestions for using New Pig products. They even got a few customers to pose for photographs with real pigs. But the really neat thing was when customers started getting into the act without being asked.

One lady got married in her pig hat. Another customer requested pig hats for his company softball team. People started taking pictures of

The 2005 Pigalog celebrated the company's 20th "Hamiversary" with more than 4,500 spill containment products. Courtesy of New Pig Corporation. Used with pigmission.

themselves in pig hats while on vacation and sending them to their customer service rep. One even snapped a shot of New Pig socks being used to stop window leaks at the Palace of Versailles in France.

So you see, much like Harley Davidson's passionate hog owners, New Pig has cultivated a legion of enthusiastic hog lovers, too—170,000 of them in 40 countries. But don't get the idea that silliness is all you need for success in this or any other business.

THE NEED TO BE TWICE AS GOOD

Behind the scenes, New Pig is all business. The company has invested millions in inventory and data management systems. And if you go to its Web site (www.newpig.com), you'll find technical papers, application bulletins and government regulations on everything related to spills and handling of hazardous materials.

"We have to be twice as good because of our fun image," said Nino Vella, president and CEO. "The brand image keeps people coming back and gives us the benefit of the doubt if there's ever a problem. And it makes it easy for customers to recommend us to others."

"But we still have to perform to the highest possible level," he continued. "Leak and spill containment is a serious business, and if you want to be seen as the leader, you have to deliver quality products in a timely and professional manner."

Along with New Pig's huge database of active customers, Vella says the New Pig brand is the Company's No. 1 asset. "It gives us an expectation of future sales, and that's like money in the bank," he added.

And with annual sales now exceeding $100 million, I'd say that's definitely something to squeal about.

Portions of this case study are reprinted with permission from *Marketing News*, October 27, 2003.

CASE STUDY 19

IN THE PINK: THE OWENS CORNING STORY

What would you say if your ad agency wanted to make a recommendation to the CEO for the company to hire SpongeBob SquarePants as your new corporate spokesperson? And would it make any difference if your primary product was yellow in color?

You can probably imagine then the panicky thoughts that were racing through the minds of Owens Corning marketing people back in 1980 when their agency, Ogilvy & Mather, suggested The Pink Panther was just what the inspector ordered to buff up the Owens Corning brand and separate the fiber glass insulation manufacturer from major competitors like Johns Manville, CertainTeed and Knauf.

It certainly didn't help matters when the CEO at the time, Bill Boeschenstein, said he'd never heard of the Pink Panther and wanted the agency to do some research to find out how popular he really was. He also said he would have to give the matter some serious personal thought.

But this is one of those rare occasions when the agency didn't mind having the client talk over their idea with the wife and family, because when Boeschenstein mentioned the Pink Panther at dinner that night, his kids went crazy. Even Boeschenstein's 85-year old mother knew who the Pink Panther was. They loved the possibility that he would actually hire the rascally creature and put him to work for Owens Corning.

So he did, and the rest is branding history. It's easy in retrospect to see the natural fit between the engaging Pink Panther and the one-and-only manufacturer of pink insulation. But like most brand management decisions, this was anything but easy.

TECHNICAL MANAGERS LIKE TO BE TECHNICAL

"Even today, after 25 years of successful promotions we still have some squeamishness," said Lynne Hartzell, Director of Marketing Communications and Brand for Owens Corning. "Technical managers naturally think that animated characters undermine the seriousness of their technology. And they definitely don't want to appear frivolous."

Like, for example, in Owens Corning's composites business, where advanced technology is a big part of the sale. Company managers resisted using the Pink Panther until 2004, when they finally relented in welcoming his larger-than-life presence at a major industry show in Paris where he was a huge hit—drawing attention and booth traffic from the technical crowd.

So even famous, well-established mascots take awhile to catch on everywhere. In actual fact, Owens Corning already had a mascot in 1980 when O&M made the fateful recommendation: "Pinkie" the pink teddy bear.

It was easy, however, to keep Pinkie under wraps, taking him out only for limited and very special appearances. Not too many people were even aware of Pinkie's existence, and he certainly didn't have the established international star power of The Pink Panther. So when the Panther came on the scene, Pinkie took early retirement.

THE COLOR OF SUCCESS

Since that time, Owens Corning has followed a very deliberate and consistent strategy of associating everything good in fiber glass insulation with the color pink. They even have a trademark on "PINK" for building

The Pink Panther stands tall over the Owens Corning display at a major industry tradeshow. Copyright 2004-2005 Owens Corning. The Pink Panther © 1964-2005 Metro Goldwyn Mayer Studios Inc. All rights reserved.

materials, including insulation, housewrap and packaging for shingles. In fact, Owens Corning was the first company to register a single color for any product. They are the exclusive owner of the color pink for any building material product—no other manufacturer can use that color for those goods.

Surveys show that most homeowners now think *all* insulation is pink, but that's not true—only Owens Corning insulation. It is true that Owens Corning commands a market share that is double its nearest insulation competitor.

The consistent use of The Pink Panther in Owens Corning advertising and sales promotion has separated them from the pack, and if you look on the front cover of this book, you'll see that's a pretty powerful accomplishment. "We refer to the Pink Panther as a real clutter cutter," said Hartzell. "He allows us to stand out in just about any environment."

That includes media advertising, tradeshows, point-of-sale materials, even model home displays and builder events. Sometimes it can go too far, however, like the builder who wanted to use the term, "Panther Homes" for some of his models. But most marketers don't mind dealing with problems like that. Getting noticed is Job One, and The Pink Panther does that very nicely for Owens Corning.

BUILDING A FRIENDLY, ENGAGING PERSONALITY

But their use of the Pink Panther goes much further than merely getting noticed. The Pink Panther has helped Owens Corning create a friendly, engaging personality that strengthens bonds with builders, wholesalers, retailers and especially homeowners.

Builders like putting Pink Panther graphics on their trucks and using Pink Panther paw tracks to guide potential home buyers into their model homes. Big box retailers like Home Depot and Lowe's use Pink Panther point-of-sale materials and strong quality image to attract builders, remodeling contractors and DIY homeowners to their insulation product display areas.

And Owens Corning has frequently used actors and employees in Pink Panther suits to create photo opportunities at tradeshows, store openings and other P.R. events. There are 350 Pink Panther suits hanging in regional office closets and storage rooms right now, ready to go to work at the drop of a paw.

When the company became a sponsor of the post-season NIT basketball tournament, suddenly large, pink foam hands (paws?) with "we're number one" fingers extended were everywhere in the arena. Which begs the question, can panthers really have fingers?

GOING BEYOND INSULATION

More recently, Owens Corning is learning how to use Pink Panther power to promote other products beyond the obvious pink insulation base. Customer roundtable feedback has encouraged Owens Corning to use their pink mascot to promote asphalt roofing shingles, vinyl siding, acoustic systems and other building products.

When Owens Corning acquired the Cultured Stone company (through the acquisition of Fibreboard and numerous subsidiaries in 1997), the new division was using a caveman mascot called "Rocky" to promote its manufactured stone veneer products (Cultured Stone® is a registered trademark). The question was, do we keep Rocky or insert the Pink Panther? Research showed that customers and channel partners supported using the Pink Panther.

So Rocky took a seat next to Pinkie on the unemployment line bench.

REACHING OUT FOR NEW CUSTOMERS

Another problem is that Pink Panther fans are aging baby boomers. Younger home buyers are not as likely to identify with the Pink Panther as their parents and grandparents. But that problem is soon to be rectified with the release of a new Pink Panther movie starring Steve Martin and Kevin Kline. Owens Corning is preparing to jump on this bandwagon and ride it into the future.

For the first time, Owens Corning is experimenting with in-theater advertising. Lobby displays and animated theater ads will direct movie goers to a website to enter a contest to win an exterior home makeover.

"Baby boomers know the Pink Panther," said Hartzell. "The challenge for us now is to reach younger home buyers who were born after the Pink Panther became popular. This new movie is a great opportunity for us to do that."

LIVING THE BRAND

The rewards of picking a strong branding concept and sticking with it are many. Not only does Owens Corning double the sales of its nearest insulation rival, but the endearing spokespanther facilitates the introduction of new products and helps attract acquisition candidates, alliance partners

A security blanket for your homeowner's wallet.

With energy costs on the rise, savings of up to 30% on energy bills will be welcome news to homebuyers everywhere.
And that's only the beginning. Our products have been rigorously tested and certified for indoor air quality by the GREENGUARD Environmental Institute, as well. Which is why, for over 65 years, Owens Corning has been the name more builders and homeowners trust. Proving once again that It's Smart To Think PINK. To find out more, visit **www.owenscorning.com/insulationproguide** or call **1-800-GET-PINK**.

The Pink Panther not only has established Owens Corning as the leader in insulation, but also facilitates the introduction of new building material products. Copyright 2004- 2005 Owens Corning. The Pink Panther © 1964-2005 Metro Goldwyn Mayer Studios Inc. All rights reserved.

and top quality employees. Plus, it also provides a point of reference for people outside the company.

"When I first joined Owens Corning," says Hartzell, "I would invariably find myself sitting on a plane next to someone who thought we made ceramic dishes. Now I just say I'm with the Pink Panther company. They know instantly who I mean."

And they know they can expect innovative, quality products that will make their homes more comfortable. That's the positioning statement Lynne Hartzell has on her wall. And it's also the way Owens Corning conducts its business.

Branding personified in a pink animated character—pretty serious stuff if you think about it.

CASE STUDY 20

RAISING YOUR SIGHTS: THE SAS INSTITUTE STORY

In 1999, SAS Institute was already the kind of company people would do anything to work for. With sales of more than $1 billion and a loyal customer base that can best be described as a huge fan club, SAS was in an enviable position. The only problem, really, was brand image.

I'm not saying it had a bad image—far from it. SAS software was revered by customers and industry experts for database and project management applications. But it was, in the words of one observer, a "geek" brand. If you weren't an IT manager with a PhD in math or statistical analysis, you probably wouldn't have a clue what to do with any SAS product. It was like rocket science.

Even though the company had logged 23 consecutive years of revenue growth since its' founding in 1976, SAS managers knew their fate was tied to one very important customer group: the so-called "C-Level" top executives of the largest worldwide companies. And those people had no idea who SAS was.

The other problem was that departments within SAS and its many worldwide offices had considerable latitude to pursue business and manage their affairs as they saw best. This was by design, because SAS co-founder and CEO Jim Goodnight believed in letting people run with their ideas, and much of the company's success could be traced to the democratic culture that had evolved.

GETTING EVERYONE ON THE SAME PAGE

But democracy has never been a very good model for brand building, and former marketing communications manager Betty Fried knew it would take something very special and powerful to bring all these groups together in support of an integrated branding program.

So the first step was to hire Copernicus Marketing Consulting to do a comprehensive customer segmentation survey. Over 1,400 in-depth telephone interviews were done with business managers and analysts, C-Level managers and IT managers. Copernicus looked at what people thought about SAS, how they talked about the software products that SAS offered, who the decision makers were, and what the most important market opportunities appeared to be.

One of the most important findings of the research was there was no standard way to describe what SAS did. "Business Intelligence" ultimately became the phrase, but others like "information delivery" (very popular in Europe), "decision support," "business analytics" and "e-intelligence" were considered.

They also confirmed the company's strong image among IT managers, and weakness among top management-level decision makers and influencers. And they verified that top management did not regard business intelligence software to be a strategic issue at that time (even though SAS felt it was).

In mid-1999, SAS hired its first outside advertising agency, Howard, Merrell & Partners in nearby Raleigh, NC. Howard, Merrell spent the better part of a year analyzing the Copernicus research, doing some more research of its' own to provide creative direction, and consulting with SAS' large in-house marcom group on a wide variety of creative and procedural issues.

THE POWER TO KNOW

One of the first things to emerge was an eloquent slogan, "The Power To Know." "We really didn't propose it as a slogan per se," said H-M senior V.P. Mike Ganey. "It was part of a creative brief." But when SAS people saw it, they knew immediately it summed up the essence of what they did.

In fact, at the annual SAS managers meeting in December 1999, Jim Goodnight stood up in front of a thousand people and said, "This is our brand promise." And from that day on, it was.

During the following year, Howard, Merrell worked with the SAS in-house group to bring the brand promise to life. One important step was development of a new logo, which led to a long list of new formats, templates and creative approaches for everything from literature and newsletters to PowerPoint slide presentations and poster graphics.

Howard, Merrell also looked at how SAS stacked up to its closest competitors, and what messages would help bring about the awareness and image changes the company sought. "It was very difficult getting our

arms around the C-Level audience," said Ganey, "because they're such a different breed and they have so many things to worry about."

The SAS marketing team knew they had a real problem when research determined that top managers thought Microsoft Excel was the "most powerful analytical software." SAS analytical software was actually driving management decisions in ninety-eight of the *FORTUNE 100* companies, but unfortunately, SAS was invisible to top managers because its products were embedded in layers of enterprise software within a large company's IT program.

So the challenge was to find a way to get on top management's radar screen.

THE TELEVISION TEST MARKET

The first brand image advertising for SAS was a television test market program that began in January 2001. Two 30-second TV spots ran in three markets: San Francisco, New York and Raleigh (to cover SAS employees primarily and other prospects in the Research Triangle).

One of the spots utilized a "harvest" theme with office workers laboring in a wheat field. The voiceover said, "The problem is not harvesting the new crop of e-business information. It's making sense of it. With e-intelligence from SAS, you can harness the information. And put the knowledge you need within reach. SAS. The Power To Know."

The other spot used a "flood" theme with a similar message. Both were computer-animated and visually compelling. Within days, New York area SAS sales reps reported receiving phone calls from prospects they had been trying to schedule appointments with.

PHASE TWO PRINT ADVERTISING

Later in the year, a print ad campaign broke in leading business publications like *Business Week, Forbes* and *Wall Street Journal.* The creative approach was unusual in that headlines were superimposed in dramatic 4-color, black and white photos on the foreheads of male and female models, enabling us to "see" what these people were thinking about SAS software.

One typical headline was, "Opportunity no longer knocks. These days it darts past the door before you can even react." Another headline was, "Ever wonder how those people who have all the answers got all the answers?"

Within six months of the television test market launch and one month of the print advertising start, unaided awareness for SAS among senior level executives had increased 48%. During that same period, switching preference (persons who would consider changing business intelligence software vendors) increased 31% in favor of SAS.

More importantly, subsequent research has tracked important shifts in the SAS brand image. Before the branding effort, it was a geek brand. Now

This computer-animated TV spot was one of two used by SAS to reach top management targets in major cities. Copyright, SAS Institute, Inc. Cary, NC. USA. All rights reserved. Reproduced with permission of SAS Institute, Inc.

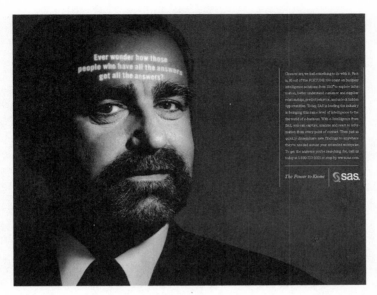

Sophisticated, thought-provoking ads like this one were used to deliver the SAS message to readers of leading business publications. Copyright, SAS Institute, Inc. All rights reserved. Reproduced with permission.

it is perceived as more of a mainstream and strategic business decision-making support brand. Before it was "hard to use." Now it is viewed as very user friendly (of course, the SAS product design people had a lot to do with that).

THE LEADER IN BUSINESS INTELLIGENCE

Before, SAS was known as a slow, deliberate company that would introduce no product before it was ready in every minute sense. Now the company is viewed as swifter and more agile, willing to take risks in order to be on the leading edge of IT development.

And as the array of new products has been received in the marketplace, the company has become known, not only as the traditional leader in business intelligence, but as the leading innovator in the field it invented.

And now, after *twenty-seven years* and the trauma of the dot-com bust, SAS has never failed to increase its revenues year-over-year. It's a business cliché, that if you're not moving forward, you're moving backward. The problem is to keep that throttle in the forward position for twenty-seven years in a row.

CASE STUDY 21

PUMPING LIFE INTO BROWN: THE UPS STORY

Many times, when a company undergoes a massive transformation, it's because something is wrong. Sales are declining or the market is drying up (see Deluxe story). Competitive pressures have infringed on your nomenclature system (see Intel). Maybe technology zigged when you zagged (see IBM).

In the case of UPS, there wasn't much wrong with the company. It was one of only eight U.S. companies with a triple AAA credit rating. For twenty consecutive years, it had been ranked as one of *FORTUNE* magazine's Most Admired Companies. In one prominent annual list of the world's strongest brands, UPS was #2 (right behind Coca-Cola).

No, UPS did not appear to be a candidate for what ultimately became one of the largest re-branding projects ever. But when you dig beneath the surface, you start to understand why it really was.

BROWN AND BORING

Looking back to the final years of the Twentieth Century, the brand image of UPS was honest, reliable, steadfast and, well, boring. In a word, it was brown. The company was also strongly identified with small package delivery. In fact, the logo designed in 1961 by famous designer Paul Rand prominently featured a small package neatly tied with a bow (see example, page 49)

Which was very appropriate in 1961. However, during the most recent decade UPS had been investing heavily in technology to speed the flow of goods, information and funds to customers around the world, and had been acquiring companies to expand its capabilities into other service areas. UPS was a lot more than small package delivery now.

Mike Eskew, who became chairman and CEO at the start of 2002, had a vision for UPS as an integrated provider of global shipping and commerce services, including supply chain management and consulting, international trade management, customs brokerage, e-commerce solutions and financial services. The UPS brand image needed to be expanded and reshaped. Customer expectations needed to be upgraded.

Another driving force for change was more mundane, but important nonetheless. It had to do with promoting the company to its various market segments in a consistent manner, with each group's messages supporting the others. "We had a potpourri of graphic systems, slogans and creative approaches," said Ed Buckley, V.P. of Brand Management & Customer Communication, "and it seemed like one group was always stepping on the toes of another, while trying not to."

With two advertising agencies and a large in-house group, it's easy to see how that could happen. On the other hand, how could you ever hope for anything better with an organization so large: 350,000 employees in 200 countries around the world, 1,748 operating facilities, 88,000 vehicles, 52,000 drop boxes. UPS was the world's eleventh largest airline with 269 jet aircraft making 1,845 flights daily to 851 airports.

Changing anything that massive would undoubtedly require an act of God. Or something close to it. But the conversations continued, and the ad managers of the three UPS business units (U.S. operations, International operations and Supply Chain Solutions), approached Eskew about the problem for the first time mid-2001 as he was preparing to step up to the chairman's job.

Eskew was skeptical about a company-wide re-branding effort, but encouraged them to continue gathering information and laying the foundation. We all know what happened on September 11, 2001. For the next few months, the question that kept popping up was, "Is this the right time for us to be spending money on something like this?"

THE GREEN LIGHT TO GET STARTED

The need to expand and reshape the UPS image, however, was not going away. If anything, it was getting more persistent. So in January 2002, after Eskew assumed the top position at UPS, he authorized the brand team to begin an exploration with a global branding firm, the internationally recognized FutureBrand consultancy. As a subsidiary of Interpublic Group and sister firm of UPS' two ad agencies, The Martin Agency and McCann-Erickson, FutureBrand seemed like a logical addition to the team.

After doing its initial due diligence, UPS and FutureBrand concluded that no terminology existed to adequately describe the unique approach UPS was applying to customers' business problems. Thus the term

"Synchronized Commerce" was coined to describe the expanded category in which UPS competes, and the phrase, "Synchronizing the world of commerce" was ultimately chosen to appear on UPS aircraft, delivery vehicles and packaging to remind customers of the company's broad portfolio of services.

WHAT CAN BROWN DO FOR YOU?

In one of those "chicken vs. egg" situations, UPS actually came up with an advertising approach that fit the new, expanded image first. They decided not to wait a year or more for the corporate identity program to be fully developed. So in February 2002, just before work on the new logo began, the slogan, "What can Brown do for you?" was introduced.

"Even though brown is not a very dynamic color, it was uniquely identified with UPS," said Buckley. "We couldn't give it up, so we decided to see if we could pump some life into it."

Making brown the focus of its new advertising program also served another purpose. Because, even though the UPS marketing group wanted to accomplish some fairly ambitious brand image changes, they were also

The "What can BROWN do for you?" slogan was introduced while work on the new UPS corporate identity program was still in progress. UPS and UPS brandmark are trademarks that are used with permission by its owner, United Parcel Service of America, Inc. All rights reserved.

mindful of the company's proud history and conservative, humble management style. They didn't want to do anything inconsistent with that, and brown provided a nice continuity device.

By the way, UPS actually has a trademark on the color brown.

THE SECRET CORPORATE IDENTITY PROGRAM

So while the company was launching its new advertising campaign, work on the corporate identity program was swinging into high gear. In total secrecy.

Basic design issues were settled by May, 2002. From September to March 2003, as many as 50 people at FutureBrand were working on UPS branding projects. Simultaneously, dozens of UPS staff members were working individually on re-branding assignments.

"In retrospect, I'm amazed we were able to keep things under wraps so effectively," Buckley said. "We had people in adjoining cubicles to our brand management group who didn't even know their neighbors were working on related projects."

On several occasions, the branding team bused CEO Mike Eskew and several of his top aides to a vacant car dealership near the company's Atlanta headquarters to show them vehicle prototypes and other graphic materials in progress.

WHAT'S IT GOING TO COST?

At some point, the brand development team had to answer the question, "How much is this going to cost?" This meant they had to recruit UPS plant engineers to the team to develop signage cost estimates. Airplane maintenance employees had to estimate the cost of repainting 269 jet planes as they were due for repainting. All 88,000 vehicles had to reflect the new graphics within 3 years. Procurement managers worked up the cost of replacing uniforms, office forms and materials that featured the UPS logo.

Buckley said the estimated re-branding costs in 2003 alone were approximately $20 million. To offset this, UPS hoped that P.R. coverage

UPS spent more than $20 million in 2003 to introduce the new corporate identity program. UPS and UPS brandmark are trademarks that are used with permission by its owner, United Parcel Service of America, Inc. All rights reserved.

from announcing the new look would compensate for a reduced ad budget, which was adjusted to offset branding costs resulting in no incremental marketing expenses for the year. (Unfortunately, the United States attacked Iraq less than a week before the external brand launch, so P.R. coverage was somewhat adversely affected.)

THE 2003 MANAGEMENT CONFERENCE

All of this effort was pointing to a key event in early 2003 that would officially kick-off the new branding program. Every year, in March, UPS brings together its top 200 or so managers for a week-long conference to discuss the state of the business. At the 2003 conference, Eskew and the brand team had a few shocking surprises for the attendees. While some knew about the branding effort, most did not.

A large tent was set up outside the conference center and UPS staged a branding exposition. Inside the tent, attendees were stunned to find UPS trucks bearing the new graphics, models of planes, signage for office and warehouse facilities, drop boxes, package delivery envelopes, uniforms, giveaways—even a redesigned NASCAR race car, the UPS sponsored #88 Ford Taurus driven by Dale Jarrett.

In the conference center, UPS managers talked about the business reasons for the re-branding program and what they hoped to accomplish. "It wasn't about graphic design or somebody's huge desire to make a creative statement," said Buckley. "It was to make us more competitive in the marketplace and help customers understand what they can expect to find at the new UPS."

The branding team wanted attendees at this conference not only to be enthusiastic about the new look, but to understand its evolution and be able to explain it to other UPS employees when they got home.

GETTING 350,000 EMPLOYEES ON THE TRUCK

Starting in Europe the morning of March 25, 2003, carefully staged employee meetings were held in every UPS location, following the sun across America and ending the morning of March 26th in Asia. Delivery vehicles that had been secretly repainted with the new graphics magically appeared, along with photos of planes and other UPS materials bearing the new graphics.

Every employee received a gift box with a logo lapel pin and a pamphlet describing some of the thinking behind the new look. Managers were provided background documents and scripted speeches to preside over these employee meetings.

"The timing was precisely controlled so that all 350,000 UPS employees could be part of a celebration," said Buckley. "We wanted them to share our enthusiasm for the new program, and they did." He said

A 50-page book titled, "UPS—a roadmap for the future" was produced and distributed to approximately 60,000 UPS managers later in the day. The book describes the concept of "synchronized commerce" and the evolution of UPS to support that strategic direction.

THE EARLY RESULTS

It's still very early in the re-branding effort, but UPS does ongoing field research with its five target audiences:

> Senior level managers
> Shipping/Logistics managers
> Front office administrators/assistants
> Small business owners
> Consumers (re UPS Store network)

On March 25 and 26 in 2003, all 350,000 UPS employees received this gift box during meetings to launch the new UPS corporate identity program. Used with permission.

What they are finding is unprecedented scores in unaided recall of UPS as a shipping resource, UPS brand attribution, and key message recall. Scores are in the 90–95% range for all three. More than 95% of respondents can attribute the advertising slogan to UPS. Moreover, UPS elevated its position from its modest and less-than-scintillating brown roots to one of a dynamic and expanding global supply chain leader.

UPS has recently announced major logistic services contracts with several prominent companies, and the Supply Chain Solutions divisional sales are up more than eight percent versus the previous year.

It's easy to see, the tightest ship in the shipping business has become a whole lot more than that.

BIBLIOGRAPHY AND REFERENCES

Aaker, David. *Managing Brand Equity*. New York: Free Press, 1991.

Aaker, David. *Building Strong Brands*. New York: Free Press, 1996.

Aaker, David A. and Erich Joachimsthaler. *Brand Leadership*. New York: Free Press, 2000.

Abrahams, Jeffery. *The Mission Statement Book*. Canada: Ten Speed Press, 1995.

Arnold, David. *The Handbook of Brand Management*. Reading, MA: Perseus Books, 1992.

Business Week "The Top 100 Brands", August 2, 2004.

Clancy, Kevin J. and Peter C. Krieg. *Counterintuitive Marketing: Achieve Great Results Using Uncommon Sense*. New York: Free Press, 2000.

Collins, Jim. *Good To Great*. New York: Harper Business, 2001.

D'Alessandro, David. *Brand Warfare: 10 Rules for Building the Killer Brand*. New York: McGraw Hill, 2001.

Davis, Scott M. *Brand Asset Management: Driving Profitable Growth Through Your Brands*. San Francisco: Jossey-Bass, 2000.

Elliott, Stuart. "IBM to transfer advertising work to single agency." *New York Times*. May 25, 1994.

Farrell, Greg. "Building a new Big Blue." *USA Today*. November 22, 1999.

Gerstner, Louis V. Jr. *Who Says Elephants Can't Dance?* New York: Harper Business, 2002.

Gregory, James R. with Jack G. Wiechmann, *Leveraging The Corporate Brand*, Chicago: NTC Business Books, 1997.

Gregory, James R. with Jack G. Wiechmann, *Marketing Corporate Image: The Company as Your Number One Product*, Chicago: NTC Business Books, 1999.

Horn, Jeffery. "The Four Lessons: Launching a corporate brand internally" Interbrand, June, 2004.

Keller, Kevin Lane, *Strategic Brand Management: Building, Measuring and Managing Brand Equity*. Upper Saddle River, NJ: Prentice Hall, 1998.

Kirkpatrick, David. "IBM: From Big Blue dinosaur to e-business animal." *Fortune*. April 26, 1999.

Knapp, Duane E. *The Brand Mindset*, New York: McGraw Hill, 2000.

Lamons, Bob. "Brick's brand mighty – yours can be, too." *Marketing News*. November 22, 1999.

Lamons, Bob. "Another story about an unlikely brand." *Marketing News*. May 27, 2002.

Lamons, Bob. "To stay in the game, stop ducking numbers." *Marketing News*. July 22, 2002.

Lamons, Bob. "The one question you should ask the CEO." *Marketing News*. June 24, 2002.

Lamons, Bob. "Beyond PR: How Hobart built expert rep." *Marketing News*. October 14, 2002.

Lamons, Bob. "Slogan crafting is truly a work of art." *Marketing News*. May 12, 2003.

Lamons, Bob. "Marcom proves itself a worthy investment." *Marketing News*. June 9, 2003.

Lamons, Bob. "Let your personality determine your voice." *Marketing News*. July 7, 2003.

Lamons, Bob. "Leverage intangible assets for improved brand valuation." *Marketing News*. September 2, 2003.

Lamons, Bob. "Even small companies can build big brands." *Marketing News*. October 27, 2003.

Lamons, Bob. "BASF uses brand power to rise above commodity logjam." *Marketing News*. March 15, 2004.

Lamons, Bob. "Brand symbols becoming a dinosaur of another age." *Marketing News*. May 15, 2004.

Lamons, Bob. "Dow Corning targets segment to keep market share." *Marketing News*. June 15, 2005.

Leavitt, Paige et al. *Business-to-Business Branding: Building The Brand Powerhouse*. Houston: APQC, 2001.

Low, Jonathan and Pam Cohen Kalafut. *Invisible Advantage: How Intangibles are Driving Business Performance*. Cambridge, MA: Perseus Books, 2002.

Maddox, Kate. "Integrated marketing success stories." *BtoB Magazine*, June 7, 2004.

Marconi, Joe. *The Brand Marketing Book*. Chicago: NTC Business Books, 2000.

Marketing Sherpa. "Using consumers to influence b-to-b buyers: How James Hardie sells 1.8 billion siding units annually." Online article. May 19, 2004.

Martin, David N. *Romancing The Brand: The Power of Advertising and How to Use it*. New York: AMACOM, 1989.

Moser, Mike. *United We Brand*. Boston: Harvard Business School Press, 2003.

Ries, Al, and Jack Trout. *Positioning: The Battle for Your Mind*. New York: McGraw Hill, 1981.

Ries, Al and Laura Ries, *The 22 Immutable Laws of Branding*, New York: Harper Business, 1998.

Ries, Al and Laura Ries, *The Fall of Advertising and the Rise of PR*, New York: Harper Business, 2002.

Ries, Al and Laura Ries, *The Origin of Brands*, New York: Harper Business, 2004.

Schonfeld, Erick. "GE sees the light." *Business 2.0*. July, 2004.

Schultz, Don E. and Heidi F. Schultz. *Brand Babble: Sense and Nonsense About Branding*, Mason, OH: Thomson South-Western, 2004.

Stein, Nicholas. "America's most admired companies." *Fortune*. March 3, 2003.

Trout, Jack with Steve Rivkin. *The New Positioning*, New York: McGraw-Hill, 1996.

Trout, Jack. "Positioning is a game people play in today's me-too marketplace." *Industrial Marketing*. June, 1969.

Upshaw, Lynn B. *Building Brand Identity: A Strategy for Success in a Hostile Marketplace*, New York: John Wiley & Son, 1995.

Upshaw, Lynn B. and Earl L. Taylor. *The Masterbrand Mandate: The Management Strategy that Unifies Companies and Multiplies Value.* New York: John Wiley & Sons, 2000.

VanAuken, Brad. *Brand Aid: An Easy Reference Guide to Solving Your Toughest Branding Problems and Strengthening Your Marketing Position.* New York: AMACOM, 2003.

Welch, Jack with John A. Byrne. *Jack: Straight From The Gut.* New York: Warner Business Books, 2001.

INDEX

About TEXERE

Texere, a progressive and authoritative voice in business publishing, brings to the global business community the expertise and insights of leading thinkers. Our books educate, enlighten, and entertain, and provide an intersection where our authors and our readers share cutting edge ideas, practices, and innovative solutions. Texere seeks to cultivate, enhance, and disseminate information that illuminates the global business landscape.

www.thomson.com/learning/texere

About the typeface

This book was set in 11 point size and Bembo font. Bembo was created in 1496 by Pietro Bembo of Italy. This typeface is known for its quiet presence and graceful stability.

Library of Congress Cataloging-in-Publication Data

Lamons, Bob.

The case for b2b branding: pulling away from the business to business pack / Bob Lamons.—1st ed.

p. cm.

Includes bibliographical references.

1. Brand name products—Marketing. I. Title: Case for business to business branding. II. Title.

HD69.B7L36 2005

658.8'27—dc22

2005016729